MW01165493

Life on the Lakeshore

The Cottage Experience

black lake
STUDIO & PRESS

Copyright © 2016 by Cottage Home

This is a work of nonfiction.

All rights reserved by Cottage Home, including the right of reproduction in whole or in part in any form.

General editorial by Cory Lakatos
Design by Caraline Visuri and Ashley Helminiak
Published by Black Lake Press of Holland, Michigan

Black Lake Press is a division of Black Lake Studio, LLC.
Direct inquiries to Black Lake Press at www.blacklakepress.com
ISBN 978-0-9913095-2-8

Cottage Home

Designers & Builders of
Well-Appointed Beach Houses & Cottages

Every Cottage Has a Story

Nowhere in the world is quite like the Lake Michigan coastline. There's a texture and rhythm to life on the lakeshore that is utterly unique. Sand, water, and sky meet in a stunning display of beauty. Charming, friendly communities gather around this natural marvel to enjoy all that it has to offer, and the jewels of the coastline are the lakeshore cottages. These homes are unique portals to the lifestyle of the Big Lake. From New Buffalo to Holland, lakeshore cottages provide unparalleled access to the richness and beauty of the beach and the surrounding communities.

But how do families come to own a Lake Michigan cottage? As designers and builders of well-appointed beach houses and cottages, we at Cottage Home have had the privilege of guiding many families on their journey to life on the lakeshore. Every story has its own twists and turns, but we have found that most take similar paths to their spot on the lake.

Dream: Childhood dreams, long-held desires, or the need for escape attract people to the Lake Michigan coast.

 Location: They find a place on the lakeshore that captures their imagination and suits their unique needs.

 Decision: With Cottage Home's help, they acquire the property and commit to making their dream a reality.

 Design: They work with Cottage Home to design a home that fits their family, lifestyle, dream, desires, and land.

 Build: They interact in a fun, stress-free way with the Cottage Home team while their home is being built.

 Move-In: In a surprisingly short amount of time, the house is finished and they are given the keys to their dream home.

 Life on the Lakeshore: The family spends time in the home and on the beach, making priceless memories.

 Aftercare: Cottage Home takes care of the family's needs long after their cottage is finished.

 Community: The family gets to know and love their neighbors and the nearby towns.

 Legacy: Their lakeshore cottage delights and enriches their family and friends for generations to come.

This book tells the story of building a home on the lakeshore by chronicling the stories of nine families who worked with Cottage Home to make their dream of living on the lakeshore a reality. Along the way, we'll dwell on some of the elements that make their homes and the surrounding communities special. Feel free to flip through this book, drinking in Lake Michigan's beauty and getting a sense for what life on the Big Lake is like. Every story is different, but the lake has enriched the lives of everyone who calls it home or home away from home. Through these stories, we invite you to begin your own lakeshore story.

Dream

"We've always been drawn to the lakeshore area, and since childhood we've both been drawn to water. The beach was always the vacation spot in both of our families. We really got hooked on family vacations at the beach, and it made us think about buying a lakeshore cottage of our own, a place where everyone could be by the lake together."

— Anthony and Jenny Iaderosa

Dream

Every lakeshore story begins with a dream, a longing for the lakeshore. The Big Lake draws people in, attracting them from far beyond Southwest Michigan.

Life can be hectic and frenzied, and it's only natural to long for a place where the craziness fades away. People seek out the lakeshore to find a spot to relax, a place where they can leave their worries behind and simply enjoy themselves.

Some people have fond memories of summer weekends on the beach when they were kids. They dream of recreating these priceless memories with their own children and grandchildren. Others remember more recent family vacations on the beach. They would love to leave behind the hassles of renting beach houses and have their own cottage and private beach where they can gather together family and friends for fun and fellowship.

Lake Michigan's stunning beauty calls to all these dreamers. Their journey begins with this longing, which sets them on the path to owning a lakeshore cottage of their own.

"Sadly, we had to say goodbye to grandma's cottage. But somewhere in the back of her mind, Jane said, 'Maybe one day we'll have our own.'"

— *Jane and Steve Marks*

"We've wanted to build on the lakeshore for at least twenty years."
— Bob and Bridget Tolpa

"I call the beach glass I collect 'treasures,' and it reminds me to treasure every day, and to treasure my family, because you don't always stop to think about those things during everyday life."

Family Name
The Marks

*Number of Stairs
to the Beach*
Sixty-three

Location
Fennville, MI

Passions
Arts and Crafts, Golf,
Beach Glass

Jane and Steve Marks' Story

Dream

When Jane was growing up, her grandmother had a cottage on Portage Lake in Manistee, Michigan. Her father and grandfather had built it, and all ten of her cousins gathered there every summer with their parents. Some of her cousins were often out of the country with their father, who was an ambassador, so it was wonderful that everyone could gather together in Michigan every year. We're still not sure how the parents did it with ten kids! They used to tell the youngsters to go out on the water to catch perch for dinner.

But Jane's grandmother had to sell the house when Jane was in graduate school, and she didn't have the money to buy it. Her father didn't want it, and Jane's efforts to cooperate with her cousins to purchase the cottage didn't go anywhere. Sadly, they had to say goodbye to it. But somewhere in the back of her mind, Jane said, "Maybe one day we'll have our own."

Location and Decision

Thirty years later we had moved to the northwest suburbs of Chicago, and we decided that it might be nice to have a vacation home. Initially we looked in both Wisconsin and Michigan, but after a couple of weeks Jane said, "Let's stop looking in Wisconsin—my heart is in Michigan." We weren't familiar with this part of the lakeshore, though we had driven past it a few times. We even thought about finding a place on Jane's grandmother's lake in Manistee.

The very first cottages we found on the Internet were ones built by Cottage Home, in a neighborhood called Summers Gate. Cottage Home did several houses there on a bluff facing Lake Michigan, and several more bordering a forest preserve. Jane was ready to buy a lot there, even though it wasn't on the lake; she said we could still walk down to the lake to watch the sunsets. But Steve wasn't convinced, so we kept looking.

"The previous owners told us there was a time capsule in the fireplace, and they asked us to find it. Brian and the gang painstakingly dismantled the fireplace, but they never found that time capsule. However, they did find a 1941 license plate, which we've kept."

Location and Decision, continued

The more we looked, the more we were drawn back to Cottage Home's work. We have a small family, so we were looking for something modest in size and expense. One day, Brian told us he might have exactly what we were looking for, and he showed us a property with a house on it that had been built in the early 1940s. We knew at once that it was a teardown, which was really hard for Jane, with her memories of her grandmother's cottage. She didn't want anyone else's childhood memories torn down. But we decided to go ahead.

Design

Cottage Home helped us select the lot and choose a plan for the cottage, but we ran into some issues with the homeowners association. At first they were against taking down the old cottage and building one with two floors. They were also concerned about how much water we would use. Brian worked on our behalf, convincing the association to change some of their rules.

Brian already had a plan for the site, and we liked it, so we didn't really go through a full design process. There were a few specific things we wanted, though. Jane asked for a fireplace, and Brian added that to the plan. Otherwise, we didn't change anything. We did have a few meetings about interior decorating, but that was easy, since we liked Cottage Home's other houses so much. Jane took input and inspiration from Cottage Home and did most of the decorating herself. It was a piece of cake.

Build

We had built a house in Connecticut, and it was a terrible ordeal. We were a bit leery about building again, but working with Cottage Home was the complete opposite of our previous experience. It was perfect. We live three hours away, but they were constantly sending us photos. They even did a demolition tape and a time-lapse video of the construction for us. All the window treatments were made by a friend back home, but she never came here, and she needed exact measurements. We have pictures of Jeremy holding a tape measure because we needed to be sure. Cottage Home was just fantastic. We wanted the process to be simple, so we were very hands-off. We didn't want any pink in the fireplace masonry, so they just put up a big sign there that said "No Pink Rocks." It was very simple. We had such faith in everything we'd seen them do that we were comfortable from start to move-in.

Move-In and Aftercare

Since moving in, we've been very impressed by how much Cottage Home cares for their product. Their cottage watch program is fantastic. My friend down the street had to find someone to do that for her, but it was built into our plan. It's so nice to have someone here once a month to check in. I don't believe they've ever found anything amiss with anything that they've done. Brian and the team's commitment to the house is amazing, and their commitment to the homeowner is outstanding.

A few weekends ago we received a call from Ross, who had noticed that a tree was down in the road and was blocking the way to our cottage. Of course, we were planning to come up and have people over that weekend. We got up there, parked in the neighbor's driveway, and called to ask if Cottage Home could do something about it. They said, "Sure!" A bit later, Jane decided to walk over to talk to our neighbor, just to make sure she hadn't arranged for someone else to take care of the tree. So Jane went next door, and when she came back, Ross was there cutting away at the tree! He totally ruined his chainsaw, but he got it out of the way so our guests could get through. That's just the sort of thing that Cottage Home does.

Life on the Lakeshore

Jane has rediscovered collecting beach glass. She also collects driftwood and uses it to make mobiles. On top of that, she collects Petoskey stones. Steve didn't know about any of these things, so it was fun for Jane to introduce him to all of it. Now we're down on the beach together collecting beach glass, which is really a lot of fun.

We often see wild turkeys, deer, and migrating Monarch butterflies around the house. We've even spotted bald eagles! And there's a gazillion stars in the sky, with hundreds of lightning bugs on the bluff at night. This is stuff we just don't see in the suburbs of Chicago. It's lovely.

Steve works really hard in the big city, and then he comes to the cottage and just relaxes. He'll actually read a book or take a nap on the beach, things he could never do back home. It's totally relaxing for Jane, too. She likes to say to her friends, "Should I care that I don't care?" When you're on the lakeshore, you don't care what you look like, don't care if your hair is a mess, don't care if your toenails are painted or not. There's no need to think about stuff like that. We tell our friends, "Do whatever you want—there are no requirements. Just relax, enjoy, and do whatever makes you feel good."

"This is stuff we just don't see in the suburbs of Chicago."

"Just relax, enjoy, and do whatever makes you feel good."

We have two kayaks and a paddle board, though we haven't learned how to use it very well yet. Our neighbor tells us that you just have to relax and become one with the board; maybe we need to heed our own advice and just relax more! Unlike the lake up in Manistee, Lake Michigan is warm enough in summer to swim in. Sometimes, we'll even walk barefoot on the beach in the fall. We never expected to use the beach as much as we do.

Our cottage is up on the bluff, and there are sixty-three stairs in four levels that take you down to the shore. We can walk for three miles south, most of the time without getting wet. The only reason we haven't gone further is because we know we'll have to walk back. We see plenty of other people going up and down the beach, and they often have dogs, who absolutely love it. Everyone is fine with dogs on the beach as long as their owners clean up after them.

We always take time to watch the sunset. We keep an eye on the clock, depending on what we're doing, and make an event of it. And the lake is even more dynamic in the winter. It changes from day to day, hour to hour. The sand changes every day. You never know what you're going to find. Jane finds water comforting, so to just be able to sit here and look at it is soothing.

Community

Discovering the area has been wonderful. There's a wonderful artistic community here. We love that we're halfway between South Haven and Saugatuck—it's the perfect location, in our opinion. Saugatuck is especially good for art, including craft shows. Jane has been taking a mosaic class in Barrington for five or six years. The women have all gotten really close. It's more like coffee and chitchat a lot of the time. They even decided to hold an art weekend in which half of the group stayed at our cottage and the other half stayed at our friend's cottage five miles down the road. That was really fun.

We've discovered several wonderful wineries nearby, and we like to take guests to visit them. There are a ton of fun things to do in the area. We love the corn maze at Crane's—it's really fun! And sometimes we even zip to Ann Arbor for a game at the University of Michigan, since Jane went to U of M as a graduate student.

We always appreciate getting away from the madness of Chicago. Trying to go to the fireworks in Chicago is just crazy and crowded, but it's not like that in Saugatuck. Sometimes we even avoid going into town in favor of staying at the cottage. On the Fourth of July we just sat here on our beach and watched other people set off fireworks. We could even see some of the fireworks from South Haven. It was great! We were worried about it being crowded when we went to Douglas for the Halloween parade, but we found a parking spot very close to the festivities, and we were there in about a second. It was fun and hassle-free.

Legacy

Life on the lakeshore is coming full circle for Jane. When she was a kid at her grandmother's cottage, they'd get in the car and drive to the shore of the Big Lake to watch the sunset. Having a cottage on Lake Michigan is a bit different than visiting her grandmother's cottage on an inland lake, but we get to watch the exact same sunset.

Jane is teaching our daughter about the beach glass, Petoskey stones, and driftwood she found as a child in Manistee, the items she's once again collecting on the Lake Michigan shore. She hopes that her childhood memories will become our daughter's too, now that she can walk the shores of the Big Lake and collect her own treasures.

Every year we invite our neighbors from Chicago to visit, and their visits have fallen into a predictable pattern. One family comes for Fourth of July, another for Labor Day weekend, and another on Columbus Day. Steve's family all came last summer; they're scattered across Virginia, Florida, and Maryland. Jane's siblings have come from Massachusetts, Texas, and Colorado. We'd love to host even more people here.

For now, we still live in Chicago. When Steve retires, we might move up here full-time, or maybe half-time. Steve loves to play golf and be active outside, and Jane is perfectly happy staying inside and doing her crafts. Our cottage is in the perfect location to accommodate both of our needs.

"Steve and Jane came to a number of our open houses, and they were getting very frustrated by their inability to find what they were looking for within their budget. One day at an open house they told me that the view over the lake was the most important thing to them. I said, 'If we can find you that within your budget, would you be ready to finally go for it?' They said yes, so I said, 'Follow me!' We walked over to a neighboring property, a small lot with a cruddy old cabin on it. I pulled out a plan for a beautiful little cottage on that site, which we'd already prepared. And they just said, 'Absolutely!'"

—*Brian*

"The first Cottage Home houses we saw sold us. We loved the houses, the designs, the look and feel, and the quality. And every person we talked to said we wouldn't be sorry if we built with them."

Marks' Family Cottage Profile

Steve and Jane built a cottage on a quaint, quiet little dead-end street in Fennville. The neighborhood is full of older, nostalgic cottages, giving the Marks' the authentic cottage experience. They also have a finished outbuilding with a loft for extra living space.

"People comment on how quiet and warm it is in the cottage, even when the wind is blowing."

"Cottage Home started building
in November and were finished in
March. They're amazing!"

"The Marks family's house was one of the first jobs I worked on at
Cottage Home. I like checking the weather all the time, and they put
a weather station on the roof. I got to help the electrician put that
on there, and I'm not extremely afraid of heights, but it was extremely windy. We got up on the peak of the roof, and I froze. I told
the electrician that I couldn't get any farther—I need to get down!
It was funny."

— Eric

The Southwest Michigan Land Conservancy

The goal of the Southwest Michigan Land Conservancy "is to protect the diversity, stability, and beauty of Southwest Michigan by preserving our natural and scenic lands." Cottage Home is grateful to be a part of an organization that helps to make Southwest Michigan such a great place to live and vacation. We've even helped out with the building of a trail and bridge in a new nature preserve, providing labor and materials. We heartily recommend visiting any one of the Land Conservancy's numerous, beautiful nature preserves to walk, cross-country ski, or snowshoe. We also encourage everyone who loves Southwest Michigan to become a member of the SWMLC and help to further the cause of this great organization.

"Cottage Home is involved with the Maritime Museum and the Land Conservancy, so when we moved in they gave us a year membership to each, which is really great."

— Jane and Steve Marks

"We've done some joint events with the Land Conservancy to help them fundraise. The land here is a precious resource, and we want to help them make it better."

— Brian

The Marks Family's Loft

In addition to their lakeshore cottage, the Marks family also built an outbuilding further away from Lake Michigan on the same property. Initially, the space above it was left unfinished and pre-designed for available expansion. A few years later, they called Cottage Home and asked if it could be finished by Memorial Day. It was. It's within easy walking distance of both the main cottage and the beach, and it's beautifully furnished to provide extra living space for guests.

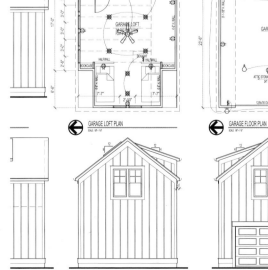
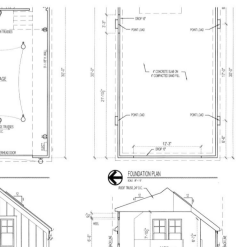

GARAGE LOFT PLAN

GARAGE FLOOR PLAN

FOUNDATION PLAN

The Michigan Maritime Museum

Cottage Home has a close partnership with the Michigan Maritime Museum in South Haven. This institution of maritime research, preservation, and education is open seven days a week in the summer, offering unforgettable experiences of the maritime heritage of the Great Lakes. The museum features exhibits on Michigan's maritime history, teaches boat building and other nautical skills, and hosts waterfront festivals and events. Historical replica ships, harbor cruises, and tall ship sailing all provide interactive ways to engage with the area's rich maritime tradition.

"Bob's a board member for the Michigan Maritime Museum. We're now involved in the community for the first time in our lives. Our jobs had never allowed us to get involved in the places we were living before."

— Bob and Bridget Tolpa

"We've worked a ton with the Maritime Museum. We had a huge gala event several years back promoting green construction on the lakeshore, and we raised $30,000 for the museum."

— Brian

Josh Kuhn

Cabinetry and Woodworking

"Woodworking started out as my hobby. I started out with bowls and pens and that sort of thing when I was about ten, and I gradually worked my way up. I learned a lot about cabinets from another guy who was doing them for Cottage Home. It's all I've ever done. It's what I like."

"We love building houses on the lakeshore! I'm from South Haven myself."

"Everybody at Cottage Home loves what they're doing. They pour their own personal passion and love of their craft into their work."

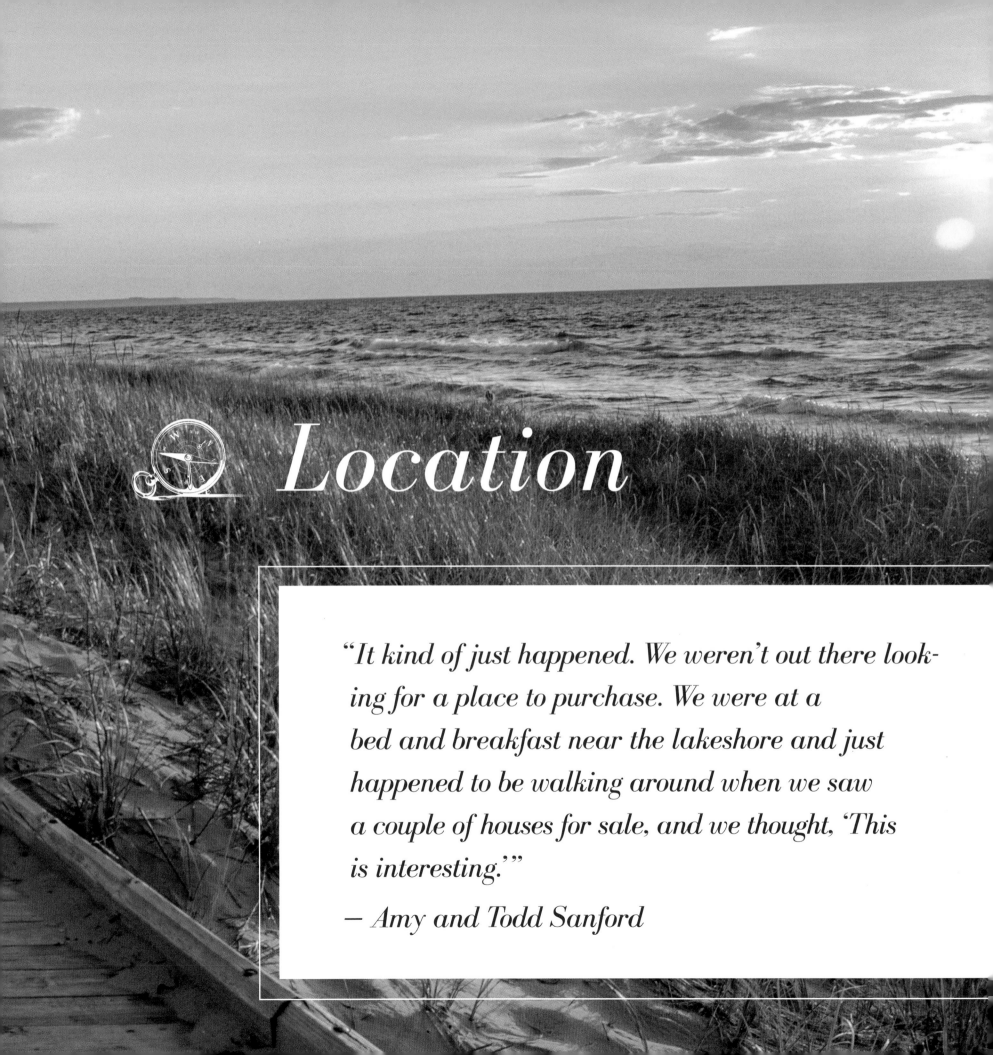

Location

"It kind of just happened. We weren't out there looking for a place to purchase. We were at a
bed and breakfast near the lakeshore and just
happened to be walking around when we saw
a couple of houses for sale, and we thought, 'This
is interesting.'"

— Amy and Todd Sanford

Location

Once someone has been drawn to Lake Michigan, they need to find a piece of the lakeshore to call their own. Cottage Home often helps clients find the right property, one that will fit all their wants and needs. What kind of neighborhood do they want to live in? Are they looking in South Haven, Fennville, Holland, or another lakeshore town? Do they want a bluff or not? We're happy to help clients find the answers to all these questions and more.

Each lot on the lakeshore is unique, with its own outstanding features and challenges. Lake Michigan dunes are sensitive environments, so Cottage Home makes sure to help clients honor the land as they're choosing a lot to build on.

Some people search deliberately, knowing exactly what they want. Others aren't so sure. They might even stumble upon the perfect lot when they're not looking.

Some seekers instantly fall in love with a piece of land. Others take more time to make a decision. Either way, their search ends with the perfect stretch of Lake Michigan beach for their family.

"*We got there just as the sun was setting. How do you go back once you've seen something like that?*"

— *Anthony and Jenny Iaderosa*

The Iaderosa family's back yard features a walkout, patio, hot tub, pool, and a fire pit on the bluff.

Family Name	Location
The Iaderosas	South Haven
Passions	*Features*
Family Reunions, Skiing, Small Town Atmosphere	Bunk Room, Bluff-Top Fire Pit

Anthony and Jenny Iaderosa's Story

Dream

As far back as when we were dating, the two of us would stay with friends in Saugatuck or other Lake Michigan beach towns. We've always been drawn to the lakeshore area, and since childhood we've both been drawn to water. The beach was always the vacation spot in both of our families. When our kids were young, we would rent houses in Michigan City or Holland for a week or so during the summer. Often, we would invite our parents or other family members, or we'd have some friends join us for a day or two. We really got hooked on that, and it made us think about buying a lakeshore cottage of our own, a place where everyone could be by the lake together.

Location

After a couple of years of renting, we decided to look for a beach home to purchase. Our search began because a friend of ours told us about a home his brother-in-law was selling. Our friend knew we had rented homes on the lake,

and he thought we might want to check it out. We'd talked about looking for a long time, but this finally lit a fire under us. We wouldn't have started looking in South Haven if it weren't for that connection. Jenny had also been attracted to Holland when we'd rented there, so we looked in that area, too. We live in Illinois, so it was about a two-hour drive. At first we thought about looking at houses on both Lake Michigan and Lake Macatawa, the inland lake in Holland, but we preferred the Big Lake. With South Haven and Holland in mind, we made plans to see some houses.

This was in 2008, so the economy was in a bit of trouble, and we were looking to see if we could find something below market value. We didn't even know that Cottage Home existed, but the night before we were going to drive up to South Haven, Anthony got online to see if there were any other homes we should look at. Ironically, the listing for the property that we now own had just gone up that day.

> *"We walked out onto the property and knew instantly that there was no turning back. We looked at each other and said, 'This is it!' We'd never seen anything like it."*

Location, continued

It had a drawing of a small home and said, "Live in the guest house while you design your dream home." The property was out of our price range, but he printed it out jokingly and showed it to Jenny.

We didn't think we would look at it, but we had a bit of spare time after looking at other houses the next day, and we figured there was no harm in looking. We got there just as the sun was setting. We walked out onto the property and knew instantly that there was no turning back. We looked at each other and said, "This is it!" We'd never seen anything like it. We'd seen and stayed in a lot of places that were on a high bluff, but this property wasn't, and that was unique. The other thing we said to each other was, "Oh, now we're in trouble!" How do you go back once you've seen something like that?

Decision

We got in touch with Cottage Home the very next day. Anthony went to their website while he was at his office and found a video called "Your Summer Story." He'd decided in his own head that he wanted to move forward, though we were still going back and forth on it, so he called Jenny at home and said, "I don't want to do this to you, but watch this video and then call me back." Well, Jenny watched it—it's an inspiring video of families on the beach—and then called Anthony back ten minutes later, crying: "You call them and tell them we'll take it!" We were very moved by the stories of people like us who had built with Cottage Home and had their lives changed for the better. We were ready to begin.

Design

We sat down with Brian for several hours, and it was a very unique experience. He didn't want us to come in with blueprints or pictures out of magazines. He just wanted us to show up, and he was going to talk to us about how we live and what our families are like. Based on that information, he would extrapolate what we needed in a cottage, and then he would put something on paper and present it to us. Honestly, we were a little worried; every other time we'd built the process included looking through books and plans, showing the builder what we liked. We sat down with Brian and he asked us questions like, "How many people do you usually have over for dinner? How large are your families and friend groups? How many children will be around?" These weren't the kind of questions we expected a homebuilder to ask us. But the meeting went really well, and two or three weeks later we went back up to their office, wondering, "How's this going to work?" The drawings that Brian showed us at that meeting are 95% of what our house is right now. We didn't change very much at all. Brian was very insightful. It was perfect.

We were pretty hands-on during the rest of the design process, and they made it really easy for us. We'd get our kids off to school, get in the car, and drive up to Cottage Home's downtown Holland office for a design meeting. They have a room with all the different selections, and they would lay out samples of plumbing, tile, or whatever we were deciding on that day. We would go through the selections, they would make suggestions and offer us alternatives, and we would make our choices. Then we would break for an hour so they could clear out the room and bring in different samples. They suggested we walk down the street, have lunch, talk about our selections, and then walk back for another session. It was so nice and seamless.

> *"Cottage Home is there from A to Z. If you don't even have a lot yet, we can help you with that. We can help you pick out colors, furniture, everything. We can handle any minor issue that you have. We don't just offer the house—we offer the total package."*
>
> *—Justin*

"It was so nice and seamless."

"The view is just amazing!"

"You feel like you could be on the Mediterranean, you could be anywhere, when you look out over the lake. You can see water from every window, every single room. It's like being in a boat."

Build and Move-In

When we built our house in Illinois, there were some hiccups in the process and some issues with the builder. As a result, Jenny was a bit skeptical about building a house from two hours away. We were worried that we would visit the construction site and something would be wrong, and they would be way past the point where they could change it. But Cottage Home was great about communication, keeping us in the loop with details all the time. They emailed us drawings, answered our questions, and were very thorough from start to finish. They made it so easy for us.

When we got started, the Cottage Home team told us, "We've got everything, we're ready to go, and you should plan on being in your house on April 6." We said, "Real funny—like you know the exact day already?" And they said, "Yes, we actually do. We have everything down almost to the minute." They showed us on their computer: on this day, our front door would be delivered at 9:00 a.m., and at 9:30 the carpenter was scheduled to hang it. They had everything scheduled out to the half hour months ahead of time, and they were right! They actually delivered the house a week early!

Life on the Lakeshore

When our children were younger, we'd go up to the cottage for most of the summer, definitely all of July. We'd move in for the entire month and invite friends up to visit us. Now that our kids are getting older, it's a little more difficult to spend that much time at the cottage, but I'm sure those days will come back eventually.

We mostly go up to the cottage in the summer, but we do go up in the winter as well. Every year we leave on December 26 and stay through New Year's. We invite friends and their families, and our kids bring friends. It's become a winter tradition. There's a little ski resort in Otsego called Bittersweet, and we've probably taught twenty of our kids' friends how to ski there. It's been great for my kids and their friends. It's a great memory. I like that this ski resort is small, friendly, and easy. It was a great place to teach our kids how to ski.

Community

We love the restaurants in town. Everyone is so friendly—it's so different from Illinois. In South Haven, I feel like everyone knows us. It has that small town feel. When we go out to dinner, the owners of the restaurants know my kids' names, and my kids love that. They feel like they're special, almost like celebrities, because of that small town feel. It's a different speed, a little slower. You take a little more time and enjoy simpler things, which we appreciate, and we like that our kids get to experience what it's like to live in a small town. It's great for them to have that kind of exposure; otherwise, they wouldn't even know that it existed. We were so pleasantly surprised. Even when you go to the grocery store, everyone's just so friendly and nice. It's a completely different feel than the city.

Legacy

We used to rent beach houses for our family reunions, and it was tough with that many people (there are more than thirty of us). But now that we have this place, every year it's a foregone conclusion that we're getting the family together the week after Fourth of July. It's been great. The house has become a gathering place for both sides of our family. In fact, we have a reunion of one kind or another pretty much every weekend during the summer. We get our high school friends up there one weekend, and our college friends the next. Before we owned our cottage, it was tough to see our friends, and we never really saw their kids. But when you spend a weekend together and everyone brings their family, you can have a different kind of relationship. You get to know your friends' children. It's wonderful.

"We developed the entire private road that created seven lakefront sites. The Iaderosas' site was somewhat challenging because it was next to a park. We actually helped the township create that park, which had been an illegal public access. It was rewarding to take something that was misused and make the community better. We felt responsible to fix that first before we built."

—Brian

"We didn't have any ideas set in stone when we first sat down with Brian. We liked that Cottage Home came up with great ideas that we would never have come up with on our own. The changing rooms, the overall layout, and several other ideas were the result of their expertise building on lakefront property."

Iaderosa Family Cottage Profile

Anthony and Jenny purchased this property just after Cottage Home built a guest house on its eastern side. They were just in time to design and build a main beach house to be exactly what they wanted. They can sleep tons of people between the two houses, and they often have lots of family and friends visit on the weekends.

"We have a bunk room with bunks in a semicircle with a sunken sofa in the floor. It's a very unique feature of the house, and the kids just love it. There are eight bunk beds, but we have like eighteen kids sleeping in there because everybody wants to sleep in the bunk room. So we'll have them sleeping on the floor or anywhere they can."

"You can completely rely on Cottage Home. We wouldn't build a house with anyone else. With them, it gets done and it gets done right. You can put absolute faith in them. They get it. You can tell them something and they completely understand. We've never had an experience like that with a builder. We've said so many times over the year, when we've needed something done at our other house, 'Why can't there be someone like Cottage Home here?' And even beyond that, we've used Cottage Home as a metaphor for people who get it and get it done: 'I wish there was a Cottage Home of...' whatever. It's incredibly unique."

"It was rare to have a property where we could have a guest cottage, so we wanted to take advantage of the opportunity. We did all the setup and the utilities so a future beach house could be built, but the guesthouse was the first phase. It was a significant invest-ment, and we had never heard of anybody doing that, but we thought it would work."

— Brian

Orchards, Farms, and Wineries

West Michigan is well known for its local agriculture. Fresh fruit is abundant in late summer and autumn. Crane's Orchard in Fennville has apples, peaches, and cherries that you can pick yourself, plus fun activities for kids and adults. There are also many blueberry farms in the area. South Haven celebrates them every August at the National Blueberry Festival. And don't forget about the wineries!

"We've discovered several wonderful wineries nearby, and we like to take guests to visit them. We also love the corn maze at Crane's—it's really fun!"

— Jane and Steve Marks

"I grew up on a blueberry farm, and I have my own blueberry farm, too. I love the blueberry festival in South Haven."

— Josh

Bunk Rooms

Lake Michigan cottages are privileged places for making precious childhood memories. We like to facilitate that by building bunk rooms in many of our cottages. Bunks feature personal shelves, lights, and electrical outlets so kids can read and play games before drifting off to sleep. Bunk rooms create a sense of togetherness for kids, and they're the perfect places to rest after an action-packed day on the beach.

"We love our bunk room. It's a great way to have all the kids together. I don't think we would have thought of that without Cottage Home."

— *Anthony and Jenny Iaderosa*

"We had seen Cottage Home's famous bunk rooms in their other homes, and we wanted one for our grandkids, so we had them put in six bunks. Initially it looked like we would need three ladders, but that also looked like it would take up too much space. So Jack sketched out a solution and showed it to Brian. The two of them sat down with the carpenter and designed a single ladder that's attached to the wall between the two sets of three bunks, and that's what they built. Our grandkids climb up the ladder and then use a set of handholds to swing over to the top bunks. It became a rite of passage, something that each of them was finally able to do once they got big enough. Little features like this have created great memories for our family over the years."

— *Jack and Barbara Weigle*

"Cottage Home built a flagstone walkout from our pool to the fire pit, which is on the border of our dune. Fifteen flagstones wind out of our grass and into the beach grass, and then they just stop. They pick up again with three or four more flagstones by the fire pit. We didn't understand it at first, but once we got it, we thought it was a cool touch. They constructed it a bit like an infinity pool, where it goes and then stops. Brian knew we wanted a beach house, so he drew our eyes out to the beach with those flagstones. He knew what we wanted better than we did."

— *John and Lisa Nevins*

Fire Pits

Whether it's a warm summer night or a crisp fall evening, fire pits are natural gathering places for family and friends. Some are situated near the pool, while others take advantage of the dramatic views on the top of the Lake Michigan bluff. Wherever it's located, a fire pit brings everyone together for warmth, food, and fun.

"I love our fire pit. It was a phenomenal idea, and it's an amazing gathering place. We have fires out there all the time, and we love to roast marshmallows and cook meat over the fire. People are drawn to it. You feel like you're perched above the world."

— Anthony and Jenny Iaderosa

Doug Postema

Architectural Drafting and Estimating

"I started doing architectural drafting, and then I moved more into the engineering side of things. Now I'm doing a bit of that, but more of the purchasing and estimating side of things. I'm also working on construction specifications. It all relates to the details behind the scenes of the project."

"My job's important because you have to have the details figured out before the building starts going up, otherwise it won't be a successful project. It's good to have all that figured out ahead of time."

"I love to go to the beach with my family. It's a place to relax and unwind. I don't have any worries on the beach. We like to take advantage of the resources that are close to us. And the communities in this area provide a bonus on top of the natural resources. It enhances them and provides more fun."

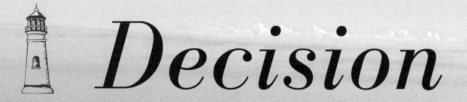 # Decision

"We'd been friends with Brian and his family for years, never knowing about Cottage Home. Then, by utter coincidence, Barbara found out that the solution to our problem had been right under our noses all along! We started to get excited about designing a new cottage."

— Jack and Barbara Weigle

Decision

Building on the lakeshore is a big decision that our clients do not take lightly. They consider their options, think about their wants and needs, and count the cost before taking the plunge.

Families who are looking for a home away from home on the Big Lake talk to other families who have built Lake Michigan cottages, including past clients of Cottage Home. They do their homework, investigating lots and builders and figuring out what design features they like and don't like. These families want to make the most of their investment, so they assess each possibility against their expectations for the perfect lakeshore getaway.

Finally, with Cottage Home's help, they acquire a lakefront property and commit to making their dream a reality.

"Anthony went to Cottage Home's website while he was at the office and found a video called 'Your Summer Story.' He'd decided in his own head that he wanted to move forward, though we were still going back and forth on it, so he called Jenny at home and said, 'Watch this video and then call me back.' Jenny watched it and called Anthony back ten minutes later, crying: 'You call them and tell them we'll take it!' We were very moved by the stories of people like us who had built with Cottage Home and had their lives changed for the better. We were ready to begin."

— Anthony and Jenny Iaderosa

"Everything just fits on the lakeshore. When people are there, they're just happy."

Family Name	Location
The Nevinses	Fennville
Fun Fact	*Passions*
They never wanted to build a house again, but changed their minds.	The Beach and Pool Lifestyle, Family Time

John and Lisa Nevins' Story

Dream

Whenever we talked about going on vacation, Lisa would always say that she really wanted to be by the water. It renews and energizes her; it's really important for her to be near water. Similarly, John was looking for an outdoor experience, a place where we could paddle board, kayak, fish, and swim.

Location

John thought it might be great to have a place up in the woods of Northern Wisconsin, but that area is too far away from us. We ended up drawing a circle around us of everything within three hours and deciding to look in that range. We quickly dismissed houses on smaller lakes in Wisconsin and Illinois for being too congested and not nearly as beautiful as what we saw up in Mich-igan on the Big Lake. We shifted our sights to Southwest Michigan, and we were really struck by the communities and houses we saw up there, especially Cottage Home's work around South Haven.

We should also mention that we did not want to build at all! We'd been burned when we built our house in Illinois, and we did not want to repeat the experience. Working with that builder was like a full-time job for Lisa, and he was slow to fix problems that came up after the home was finished. Getting a lake house was supposed to be about relaxing, and the last thing we wanted was all that angst. When we started looking at homes in Michigan, we were adamant with our realtor that we would not be building.

"We were determined not to build, but when we stepped out of the car we immediately knew we were building a house with Cottage Home right there! It was one of those moments that takes your breath away."

Decision

We looked for months, and every home we liked had been built by Cottage Home. But for a variety of reasons, the homes we looked at didn't quite fit our family's needs. Sometimes the beach was too narrow; other times the lot was too small or too big. Week after week we made the journey up to look at houses, but nothing seemed to fit.

Finally, our realtor said to us, "I think I know the kind of lot you want, and I think I know the type of house you want, based on the Cottage Home houses you've liked. I know you don't want to build, but I've got this lot that I think you should see. Just give it fifteen minutes." We said, "Fine, but we're not building!" But when we stepped out of the car we immediately knew we were building a house with Cottage Home right there! It was one of those moments that takes your breath away. We both had the same feeling: "This is perfect. This is amazing!" So we decided to give Cottage Home a call. We met with Brian within a week, and before we knew it, we were headed down the path toward building a lakeshore cottage.

Design

The first time we sat down with Brian, we were immediately confident that Cottage Home was going to build a quality house that would fit the needs of our family. He would simply talk to us and take notes. He had a really good understanding, probably a better understanding than we had, of what we wanted and what our house should look like, since he has so much experience with building for families. He was calm, reassuring, not pushing anything, just measured and confident. We threw out some things about our experience before, and he just matter-of-factly said, "Those aren't experiences people have with us." We ended up feeling way more comfortable with beginning a design process with Cottage Home than we ever imagined we could be.

Cottage Home was amazingly quick to lay out a plan with every single room and feature. They gave us some alternatives, and we'd just go through them one by one and make decisions. We were pretty hands-off during the design process, for the most part, since we were still a little shy about building. When we built our previous house, every time we said we liked something we got a change order and were charged more. We were a little worried that this would happen again, but the things we wanted were always included. There were no change orders unless we asked for them or forgot something. For example, partway through we asked for a bigger pool. We decided we wanted one big enough to swim laps in, and Cottage Home accommodated that desire.

Build

Our kids were still young, we were super busy, and we weren't able to be extremely engaged during the building process. Brian told us about clients from Missouri that Cottage Home had built for. They only showed up a couple of times, but Cottage Home was constantly emailing them photos and specs. That appealed to us and reassured us that everything would go OK without us being there all the time.

There was no mystery behind what the costs would be, and if we had questions about an addition, it wasn't like we had to pull teeth to find out what the increase would be—they just told us what it would be, and it was on us to make the decision. We appreciated that Cottage Home touched base with us on major milestones. Lisa went up a bit more often than John, who only went up a few times. Every time Lisa went up she was so impressed by what was being done that she felt like she didn't need to be there. It was getting done and it was getting done well without us having to check up on it.

The house was almost finished when we realized that it had no bathtubs, only showers. We thought that at some point little kids or older people would want a bathtub, so we mentioned it to the Cottage Home team. They agreed that it was a good point, and they were really fair about the oversight. They charged us for the tub itself but not the labor. They just figured out where they could fit it in and did it without any kind of argument, explanation, or tension. We were very pleased about that.

"The guys are always open and willing to listen to the client. We'll do what it takes. We'll go the extra mile for all our clients."

—Joel

"From Brian to Stephanie, Ross to Jeremy, everyone we've come in contact with through Cottage Home has been a pleasure to deal with. They all listen to your needs and wants and help you get there. And they're so responsive!"

"Designing and building this great beach home made us cool with our kids!"

"We threw out some things about our bad experiences with another builder, and Brian just matter-of-factly said, 'Those aren't experiences people have with us.'"

"This is perfect. This is amazing!"

Move-In

Cottage Home helped us with move-in, including selecting and bringing in the furniture. Everything was furnished and done on closing day. It was sunny and all the blinds were up when we walked in for the first time. It was another one of those heart-stopping moments: "This is one of the most beautiful things I've ever seen." The expansive visibility we have of the lake is amazing.

Aftercare

We were concerned about what might break, how much it would cost to fix, and how big of a deal it would be. Never having owned a home on Lake Michigan, we didn't understand until a few months in how strong the storms can be. But Cottage Home has years of experience and knows what materials work in such harsh weather. Our cottage stands up against heavy rains, strong winds, ice, and frigid temperatures. It's been a huge advantage so far, and we've had no problems.

Life on the Lakeshore

Building a cottage near a small town in Southwest Michigan has enabled us to have a lifestyle we simply couldn't have had before. We like to do things outdoors, but where we live in the suburbs of Chicago, you can't really do that. Beyond a few forest preserve trails, there's not a whole lot here. But up on the lake we can go paddle boarding, kayaking, fishing, and swimming, and we can play games on the beach. It's great.

What do you need to go with a fun, relaxed pool and beach lifestyle? Cottage Home had that all figured out for us. We have a pool with a fireplace nearby in a little cove. We love to get people together and sit there during the day or night. We have an outdoor shower where people can clean off after being at the beach or in the pool. We even have a pool bathroom right there. There's a storage room for all our toys right down by the pool area as well. It was nice to have all that figured out.

We love to spend the day out on the lake on our paddle boards and then come back and take a dip in the pool, make dinner, and just be outside by the fire pit. People bring their musical instruments. Our daughter and one of her friends play the guitar, and someone else plays the drums. They'll improvise a bit, which is fun.

Lisa always said that we wanted a beach house, not just a lake house, and the landscaping Cottage Home created looks like the beach. The plantings are beach grass. You feel like you're at the beach even though you're in the pool. We love the beach feeling, and we don't always have to run down to the shore to get it.

Everything just fits on the lakeshore. All the different ages come together. Our youngest is now a freshman in college, and the boys are older. They'll all invite friends, and we'll invite friends, and everyone can come together. When people are there, they're just happy. Their differences melt away. One of our kids is an athlete, one's a brainiac, and the other is more artistic, but that all fades away and they just have fun together. It's really cool.

Community

We'd never lived in a small town before, and it's been fun to come here and get to know the people who live here. It's kind of fun to learn to live in a small town. Our suburb in Chicago isn't that big, but it's part of a megalopolis. But up there you're part of a small community, and you can actually get to know people.

You might think that a good restaurant would be hard to find in a small town, but there are awesome restaurants in the area. It's great to be able to say, "Hey, we need something for dinner. Let's go to the farmers market that's five minutes away." Or you might say, "Let's go to this restaurant ten minutes from here—it's excellent." We love that.

Legacy

Our kids were all either in college or high school at the time we built, and we wanted a place that would be appealing to them and where we could get them together as just a family, away from parties, away from school stuff and jobs—a place where we could just be us together. We have a joke around our house called "forced family fun." But we don't have to force them to come to the cottage, so it's just "family fun." They actually like going up there. It doesn't mean that they don't bring their friends, and we bring our friends now, but it also gives us that ability to get away from whatever's going on at home and enjoy just us. And with the size of the house we can sleep a lot of people. There's just enough room that people aren't on top of each other. We've had a lot of guests up there, and everyone feels comfortable. There's room for everyone.

We celebrated Lisa's fiftieth birthday the year we moved into the cottage, which was really special and cool for us. We're looking forward to celebrating many more birthdays and special occasions at our lakeshore cottage.

"John and Lisa told their realtor they'd fire her if she showed them something that needed to be built, but she took a risk because they couldn't find anything that fit their needs. They looked at the site, we went back to the realtor's office, and I showed them the concepts we'd come up with. Then they asked me for some privacy, so I went out in the parking lot to wait. Just a few minutes later they called me back in, and they had only a few little adjustments. It was a done deal!"

— Brian

"What do you need to go with a fun, relaxed pool and beach lifestyle? Cottage Home had that all figured out for us."

Nevins Family Cottage Profile

John and Lisa wanted a lake home, but they definitely did not want to build. However, after a long search, they decided to build with Cottage Home. Now they love their cottage and can't believe how easy the process was.

"Cottage Home brought some boulders from a lot they were clearing to our place and used them as landscaping around the pool. It adds to the cool beach look, and it adds extra spots to sit or put out your towel to dry."

"We were surprised by how beautiful the character grade wood floors are. We were used to oak and maple, but this has a knottier look, with interesting imperfections in the wood. Plus, it's the color of sand, meaning we don't have to see the sand we track in!"

"One thing we wanted was a bunk room where we'd have two sets of bunk beds and could sleep four little kids. We'd seen pictures of other ones Cottage Home had done, and we thought they were really cute. When they were done we went in and there was a little detail I didn't think of: each bed had its own plug and light so you could just sit in bed and read or play your game and not disturb the other people."

Tilt-Up Windows

"*Amy loves the screen porch we have in the back. We have a port window, which is a signature Cottage Home feature. We also have a pulley window, which is awesome. It's right in our kitchen and looks out onto the porch. That's a really special trait to everyone who sees it.*"

— *Amy and Todd Sanford*

"We wanted a pass-through window from the kitchen to the screened-in porch so you didn't always have to walk through—someone could just pass you a drink. At first glance you might think it's just a window, but it is on a pulley. That allows it to get completely out of the way and open wide. You don't have to stick your head under anything. Cottage Home is great at following through on details like that."

— John and Lisa Nevins

"*We knew from the beginning that we wanted a pool. We had in mind a big one you could swim laps in.*"

— *John and Lisa Nevin*

Pools

Lake Michigan's beaches are truly amazing, but you might want a different kind of fun in the sun every once in a while. That's why residents build pools. Water slides, fire pits, hot tubs, and other features can turn your backyard into a beachside resort. Cottage Home specializes in building pool patios that make the most of the view.

"The beach is constantly changing, and sometimes that means shrinking. We added a pool to make up for the low years."

— Guy and Barb Calhoun

Porches, Decks, and Three Seasons Rooms

"Our house is built up off the ground a bit so you can view the river and downtown area from the porch. There's also a screened-in, rounded porch with great views. We spend the most time there as a family. On top of that is a deck with beautiful views of town, including the festivals and fireworks. It's the envy of South Haven."

— Jon and Sherri Newpol

"We told Cottage Home that we wanted lots of outdoor deck space, and they gave us over 1,500 square feet of deck! We wanted a wraparound deck from the garage in the front all the way to the walkout in the back, and they made it happen. It's great for entertaining, even including a screened-in portion for when it's raining. We also have smaller decks on the upper levels."

— *Phil and Lynn Kennedy*

"The ceilings in both the screened-in porches were really important to Bob. It looks like you're in something very rustic. Cottage Home put in the ceiling and then the guys put in two by fours as if they were roof rafters. It looks like you're in an outdoor setting. It's great to sit in there; it's a homey, cottagey feel."

— *Bob and Bridget Tolpa*

"We practically live in our three seasons room. It started out as a porch that Brian added on his own initiative after he saw how much we loved the porch on one of the houses down the street. We loved it so much that we had it converted into a three seasons room so we could spend even more time out there."

— *Guy and Barb Calhoun*

Justin Lambers

Office and Finance

"I'm the office manager, so I handle the timeline for the house. At the beginning I'll get a professional service agreement ready in order to start off the design process. Then I'll coordinate the contract documents and work with the bank to get financing ready to go. After the fact, I'm the one who sends the invoices out, and I work on payroll in the office. I mostly work behind the scenes, but I do have a little bit of interaction with the clients. Sometimes I'm the first person they'll talk to."

"I started off my career doing public accounting, but I found that it was dull. I just didn't care about the steel company I was working for. Here I'm doing the same kind of work, but I'm passionate about residential construction. I love being able to watch that process again and again. It gives meaning to the numbers that I put together."

Farm to Table Eating

In addition to being an agricultural hub, Southwest Michigan is a center for farm-to-table eating. From locally sourced restaurants to farmers markets, fresh produce and other foods are never far away. Even the beverages are local—there are a number of wineries in the lakeshore region, and this region is nationally recognized for its breweries.

One example of the farm-to-table movement along the Lake Michigan coast is Salt of the Earth, an outstanding local restaurant in downtown Fennville. This rustic American eatery and bakery sources all of its ingredients from growers within a fifty-mile radius of Allegan County. That means the menu is incredibly fresh and creative, and it changes with the seasons. It's a refreshingly unique dining experience, and we definitely recommend you give it a try!

"You might think that a good restaurant would be hard to find in a small town, but there are awesome restaurants in the area. It's great to be able to say, 'Hey, we need something for dinner. Let's go to the farmers market that's five minutes away.' Or you might say, 'Let's go to this restaurant ten minutes from here—it's excellent.' We love that."

— John and Lisa Nevins

 # Design

"Brian is a great designer and gave us lots of drawings and sketches. We're not very technical, handy, or hands-on, so we gave the Cottage Home team a lot of freedom with the design. Their interior designers are unbelievably astute, accommodating, and understanding. They really know their stuff!"

— Guy and Barb Calhoun

⚓ Design

Some Cottage Home clients know exactly what they want in a lake home, but others are less sure. They have an idea of what they want their Lake Michigan experience to be like, but they don't know what they would need in a cottage to make their dream a reality.

That's why the design process is so critical. Cottage Home's team asks a series of questions in order to figure out what a client needs in a lake house. How big is their family? Do they like to entertain? How many children or grandchildren do they have? What kind of activities are they looking forward to? How do they want to feel when they're in their cottage? Answering these types of questions will give us the information we need to come up with a plan for your cottage. Once preliminary plans are drawn up, clients give feedback and Cottage Home makes adjustments.

Some clients have a vision of what their cottage should look like, and they often want to be very involved in the design process. Others take a more hands-off approach. Either way, they collaborate with the Cottage Home team and entrust us with their dream.

"We sat down with Brian for several hours, and it was a very unique experience. He didn't want us to come in with blueprints or pictures out of magazines. He just wanted us to show up, and he was going to talk to us about how we live and what our families are like. Based on that information, he would extrapolate what we needed in a cottage, and then he would put something on paper and present it to us."

— Anthony and Jenny Iaderosa

"The lake is what brings everybody here."

Family Name	Location
The Calhouns	South Haven
Fun Fact	**Passions**
The Calhouns live here full-time now that they're retired.	Gardening, Entertaining

Guy and Barb Calhoun's Story

Dream and Location

Barb grew up in South Haven on Lake Michigan and continued staying there with her parents during college. We visited them together even before we were married, and later we started bringing our kids to their lake house. Because of this connection, we already had established relationships in the South Haven area. We even got a small house down the street from Barb's folks so we could keep an eye on them. When Barb's parents passed away, we inherited their lakefront property. Their house was a ranch-style home that had been built in the sixties, and it needed a lot of fixing up. We weren't sure what to do with it.

Decision

We considered remodeling the existing house, then thought about tearing it down and selling the northern portion of the lot. We talked with a landscaper who recommended Cottage Home; he thought a new, smaller cottage on the land could be just the thing for us. We

called Brian and discussed it with him, and he agreed to buy the north lot and build a small house there (one that wouldn't block our views, of course!). Brian was a class act and honored all of our agreements, keeping the house small and unobtrusive. Now we have neighbors who live there.

Design

When Brian came out to look at the property, he also took a good look at the existing cottage to see what features it had. Not long after that, we sat down with him on at least three separate occasions and talked things over. He's a great designer and gave us lots of drawings and sketches. We're not very technical, handy, or hands-on, so we gave Brian and the team a lot of freedom with the design. Cottage Home's interior designers are unbelievably astute, accommodating, and understanding. They really know their stuff! We didn't have much experience with decorating, but they made it a lovely process for us.

"We were still living in the Chicago area at this time, so we couldn't drive up to South Haven too often. We decided to let Cottage Home run with the building process and trust their experience. We were not disappointed!"

Design, Continued.

The interior design they created for us, with its warm atmosphere and inviting color scheme, makes us feel very close to the lake.

Cottage Home gave us our first experience with someone who builds LEED (Leadership in Energy and Environmental Design) homes, and our cottage was the first LEED home in South Haven. The design includes a tank out back that collects rainwater to irrigate the yard. The house is airtight and energy efficient, and all the materials came from within a 5oo-mile radius.

Build

We were still living in the Chicago area at this time, so we couldn't drive up to South Haven too often. We decided to let Cottage Home run with the building process and trust their experience. We were not disappointed! They were great about communication, sending us lots of photos and keeping us up to date.

We were the first property owners in our area to take the bank down (meaning re-contouring and restoring the bluff), and our neighbors didn't like the idea. They were all worried about losing their banks, so they kept them high. They pushed back when Cottage Home bulldozed our bluff down, even when we reassured them that Cottage Home had done this beautifully at other locations. Thankfully, Brian directly addressed the neighbors' complaints and buffered us from that. In the end, we're glad we were convinced to take down the bluff, because it allowed Cottage Home to do everything that they've done on our property.

Life on the Lakeshore

We now live in our lakeshore cottage full-time, and we couldn't be happier with it. The view from our home just grabs you right away. Every room has a view of the lake. In the summer, the scenery brings together sunshine and water, and it's very inviting and enjoyable. In fact, all four seasons are magnificent on the lake, especially the fall with all its colors.

Gardening is a hobby of ours, so we made sure to leave space for that. The wicked winds we get off the lake made that a bit tricky, but we figured out a good place for the garden. We also love hanging out around our wood-burning fireplace, which the team happily installed, even though it's somewhat unusual for Cottage Home. And we practically live in our three seasons room. It started out as a porch that Brian added on his own initiative after he saw how much we loved the porch on one of the houses down the street. We loved it so much that we had it converted into a three seasons room so we could spend even more time out there.

Community and Legacy

There's a lot to do in this area, which helps us encourage people to come visit us. Our cottage has become a hub for entertaining our friends. We've made a lot of great memories when our friends have visited. In fact, some of them liked our cottage so much that they've purchased their own homes in the area.

We also love it when family comes to visit. We have five grandkids, and they simply adore the beach. The beach is constantly changing, and sometimes that means shrinking, but we added a pool to make up for the low years. This is a wonderful place to spend our retirement, and we're excited to share the Lake Michigan shoreline with our friends and family far into the future.

"Barb's father was an inventor and a very practical man, and that home was not the prettiest house in South Haven! It was the width of two lakefront lots, and you could hardly see the lake because of the hedge at the top of the bluff. They were talking about a significant renovation to the house, but were wavering. I challenged Guy and Barb to start from scratch with the cottage and to reshape the bluff to be more natural. If they sold the second lot, they'd have all the revenue they'd need to build a new home. It worked out perfectly for them."

—Brian

"Barb wanted a big kitchen, so Cottage Home designed one that opens into the dining area and looks out over the lake. It's spacious, open, and inviting. But even though we wanted a big kitchen, we didn't want a huge house. This was going to be our home when we retired, so we envisioned it as more of a home than a beach house or vacation getaway."

"We couldn't be happier with our cottage."

"It's important to look at a builder's work before deciding to go with them, and all of Cottage Home's work that we saw was phenomenal. We recommend taking a look at some of their cottages—it'll give you lots of ideas for what you want in yours."

Calhoun Family Cottage Profile

Guy and Barb owned this property for years, and originally they wanted to remodel the old cottage. Eventually, they decided to tear the house down, split the property in half, and rebuild. Cottage Home also purchased the remaining parcel, built a showcase home, and sold it to another client.

"Cottage Home's interior designers are unbelievably astute, accommodating, and understanding. They really know their stuff! We didn't have much experience with decorating, but they made it a lovely process for us. The interior design they created for us, with its warm atmosphere and inviting color scheme, makes us feel very close to the lake."

"Cottage Home gave us our first experience with someone who builds LEED homes, as our cottage was the first LEED home in South Haven. The design includes a tank out back that collects rainwater to irrigate the yard. The house is airtight and energy efficient, and all the materials came from within a 500-mile radius."

Wendy Spoelhof

Interior Design and Selections

"I assist our clients in the selection of finishes, furniture, cabinets, tile and paint colors for the interior and exterior of their home. I also act as a client liaison. As the process moves forward, clients call me and tell me their thoughts and concerns, and it is my job to make sure their voice is heard throughout the whole process. I help make their ideas valuable. Listening to clients and understanding their needs is key to the design process. I want the design to be aesthetically and functionally everything that they are looking for. Most importantly, I want them to be happy with the end product and I want the process to be seamless and enjoyable."

"Many of our clients don't live in the area, so we communicate and work via email, phone calls, and texts. I make sure to find out what method of communication works best for them."

"I've lived in Holland almost my entire life, and I love lakeshore living. There are so many things you can do here, and it's beautiful all seasons of the year. We have a great community, and a lot of great things happen on the lakeshore. It's fun to live in a resort town, where some people live here year-round and others come and go. It makes things exciting."

Custom Cabinets

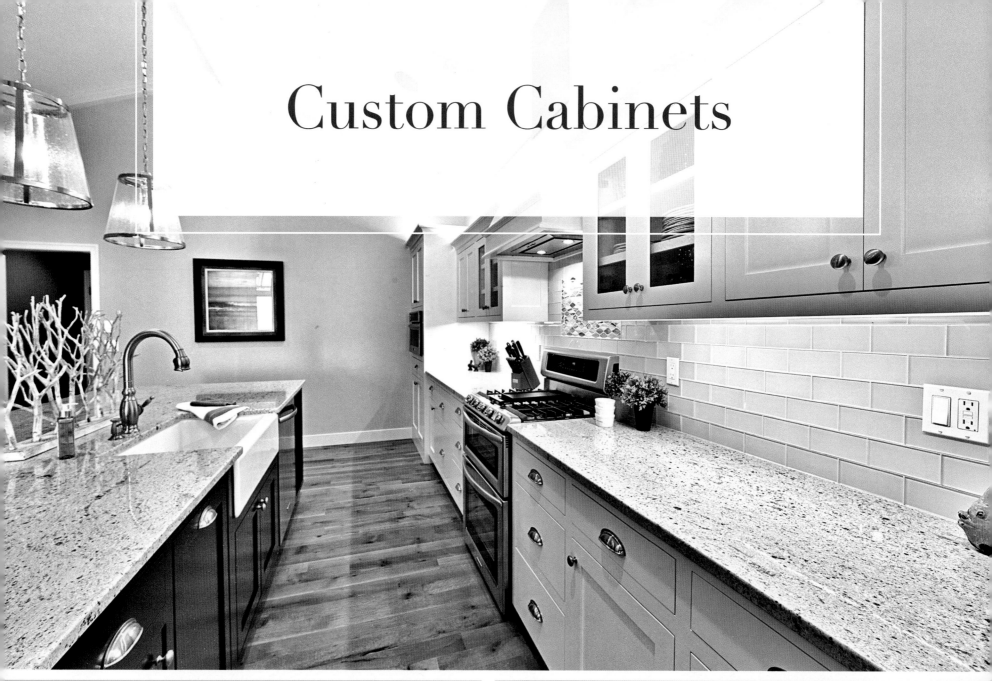

"We visited Cottage Home's cabinet shop and got to meet the guys who built our cabinets. We were really excited about that."

— *Phil and Lynn Kennedy*

"Most of the time I get to come in at the end and put in all the hardware, and it's fun to see everything come together."

— Josh

"The quality and the time we put into our houses is what defines them. We build custom cabinets, which take time and craftsmanship. They're not like pre-fabricated cabinets. Every house we go into we treat like our own house. We use high-quality vendors, and we go that extra mile to make sure it's right, and that it's done the way we want it to be done."

— Joel

The Arts

Southwest Michigan is known for its local arts scene. From arts and crafts shows and theaters to studios, galleries, and museums, the towns along the lakeshore have it all. At the heart of the regional arts scene are the Blue Coast Artists. For more than twenty years, their fall tour has given visitors and locals alike a behind-the-scenes look into the workings of area art studios. The tour covers the scenic Blue Star Highway and back roads between Saugatuck and South Haven, showcasing a distinctive, culturally diverse community of artisans. Don't miss the art-making demonstrations that show the creative process in action!

"There's a wonderful artistic community here. Saugatuck is especially good for art, including craft shows."
— Jane and Steve Marks

Saugatuck and Douglas

Known as the "Art Coast of Michigan," the twin cities of Saugatuck and Douglas more than live up to their nickname. The Saugatuck Center for the Arts holds performances, concerts, classes, and workshops year-round. The Waterfront Film Festival, featuring movie premiers, workshops, parties, and more, was named as a top ten film festival in the U.S. And in addition to the arts, these lakeside resort towns have boating, festivals, delicious local cuisine, and everything else your family needs to have a great time.

Brian Bosgraaf

President and Designer

"I really value my own experience with the lakeshore, and I like being the guide that helps other people get there. It's rewarding to help other folks find their place. I enjoy the challenge of solving the riddle of what people want, need, and can afford. I also like fixing the land, resolving the issues. Everything we come across is messed up. Everything's been touched or used or abused, and it's in our company's ethic to fix it and leave it clean, beautiful, and better than it was, both for the environment and for the owners."

"Cottage Home is important to me because growing up, my grandparents had a cottage on Lake Michigan, and it's where we all gathered in the summer. There wasn't enough room for us all to sleep overnight, but we did lots of sailing and body surfing. We'd go out in the worst storms, and I'm surprised we all lived! I made great memories with all my cousins. I was also fortunate enough to buy a cottage of my own, and it's become central to our family."

South Haven

South Haven is a small town with big appeal. Premiere local restaurants and shopping perfectly complement wineries, breweries, and a vibrant arts scene. The boating and beach life here are top-notch. And on top of all that, local festivals like HarborFest, the National Blueberry Festival, and the All Crafts Fair provide fun and excitement for the whole family.

"*After we re-contoured the Calhouns' bluff, the city of South Haven contacted us about the bluff property they own. They'd never done anything to repair the damage from erosion over time, and they had some of the nicest property on the lakeshore. We encouraged them to do a better job maintaining it. They took our advice, and now the public amenities of the City of South Haven are so much better.*"

— Brian

"*In South Haven, I feel like everyone knows us. It has that small town feel. When we go out to dinner, the owners of the restaurants know my kids' names, and my kids love that. They feel like they're special, almost like celebrities.*"

— Anthony and Jenny Iaderosa

"*I live in South Haven, and I have a boat in the harbor there. I love that lifestyle of boating and fishing on Lake Michigan. It's very seasonal, but there's something to do all the time. It's a really unique area between South Haven and Holland, very quiet and relaxing. I'm truly living the dream of living on the lake.*"

— Eric

Eric Leatherberry

Construction Superintendent

"I'm the onsite construction superintendent, and also the frontline manager between the office and the field. I make sure the guys have all the information they need to keep moving forward. Everyone on the team cares. Everybody has their own role, but we're super team-oriented. We do really unique stuff that's cool and fun, and people like that."

"*We cater to our clients from day one. Brian designs them a house, Ross takes care of things while they're not there—it's an all around catering service to the clients. That allows them to relax at the lake.*"

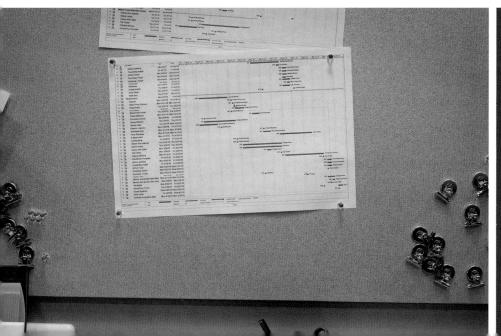

"*I love what I do, which makes it very easy to get up and go to work. I feel like we're a hospitality builder. It's all about the experience and the journey. I like dealing with people, so I love this job.*"

Build

"When we were almost done building this house, we got that horrible feeling you get halfway through a vacation. It was a great experience from the start to finish, and we didn't want it to end. We could not have been happier. Cottage Home made their deadline, and it wasn't taxing on the neighborhood like it usually is."

– Phil and Lynn Kennedy

Build

Building is the part of the process where the rubber meets the road. All of the dreaming, location hunting, decisions, and design work culminate in approximately five to six months of intense activity. For many of Cottage Home's clients, this is one of the most exciting parts of their lakeshore story. It can be deeply satisfying to watch as a cottage takes shape.

Visiting the job site energizes some owners. They stop by whenever they can to check up on progress. Thankfully, Cottage Home has everything under control and on schedule, so they need not be anxious. They can simply sit back and watch the show.

Other clients are not the type to get excited about construction, so they stand back and let our team handle things. A lot of our clients live several hours away, so they can't visit very often. We make sure to keep them in the loop, sharing photos and updates so they can follow along as their cottage nears completion.

"Our excitement was almost uncontainable. I think friends and family hid from us because we were always talking about the cottage. We came up every single weekend our house was under construction. Cottage Home figured out what we were doing after a couple of months, because we'd always send them a complimentary email. Then one weekend we found two adirondack chairs in the spot where we would sit. They gave us the chairs to keep, and they're beautiful!"

— Bob and Bridget Tolpa

"This is a renovated farmhouse that was built before the Civil War. Cottage Home originally planned to tear down both houses on this property, but when we figured out how old they were, we fell in love with them and found a way to save them."
— Brian

"There have been many times when the infrastructure wasn't sufficient for the new house, and we facilitated upgrades of the entire system. Then all the electric systems get better in the entire neighborhood. We coordinate with the power company and with the neighbors, whether it's getting Internet to the cottage or taking natural gas down there. Our work enhances the whole community."
— Jeremy

"We build creative, cool stuff. There are a million ways to build a house, but we feel that we build it the right way. I take a lot of pride in making sure everything's being done the way it should be. Our standards are very high, and quality is always a large factor. We work very efficiently as a team, and that's what really makes it all come together. I think being organized and having a plan and schedule is extremely important. Then everything clicks together."
— Eric

"We just want to stay here, and we can hardly wait to get back to the house when we do leave."

Family Name	*Location*
The Kennedys	Holland
Features	*Passions*
Walk-In Pantry, Lookout Spot, Croquet Lawn	Green Building, Quality, Croquet

Phil and Lynn Kennedy's Story

Dream and Location

Lynn was born and raised in the Holland area, and her parents moved into a home on the lakeshore in 1985. They were there for most of Lynn's adult life, and they had many gatherings with family members and friends from out of state. Lynn has a lot of family memories of the old home.

Phil grew up in Maryland, and if his family got to the beach once a summer, it was a miracle. His mom hated the traffic on the Chesapeake Bay Bridge. Then he started his ninth grade year in Newport, Rhode Island, and saw a lot more of the beach there. Now Phil doesn't feel comfortable being away from the water, and the Lake Michigan shoreline is more special to him than either of those areas.

Since Phil was in the navy and the two of us worked for an airline, we have lived all over the country. When Lynn lost her parents, we moved back to Holland but kept our house in Kansas City. Then one day we realized that we

hadn't been to our Kansas City home in four months—we'd inadvertently migrated to the lakeshore to stay. We started thinking about tearing down the old house and starting from scratch.

Decision

Lynn found an article in a magazine about Cottage Home titled "Michigan's Greenest Builder" and gave it to Phil, since green building is important to him. We wanted a house that would accommodate fifteen to twenty people, but that we could still live in when it was just the two of us. We started out by trying to get permission to build a retaining wall. The Department of Environmental Quality said we needed to find an environmental engineer who specializes in dune work, but we didn't know where to find someone like that. We thought it might be good to involve a builder at this point, so we pulled out the article and decided to give Cottage Home a call.

"The Cottage Home team were good neighbors and good stewards. They didn't want people to contact us if they had issues, so they gave out their contact information. It was pretty amazing."

Decision, Continued.

Brian came out with just a notepad, and we walked around the house with him. He realized that a spot in the back where we had a clothesline actually offered our best view, and he proposed turning the house around and setting it back so there would be great views from every room. We said that sounded beautiful!

But Lynn was scared that things were going too quickly, like a runaway freight train. Phil was very particular about what he wanted in a cottage. Quality and green building were particularly important to him. Lynn was worried that it would be hard to work with a builder because they would want to do it their way. Our neighbors, friends, and others told us not to do it. One said that building a house nearly ruined their marriage! We were uncertain when we went to Brian's office for the first time, but instead of falling behind, Brian was finishing Phil's sentences and speaking his language. He understood and appreciated quality in the same way, and Phil didn't have to educate him. Brian even told the rest of his staff that he'd just talked with "someone who gets it." It was beautiful! When we got in the car after that first meeting, we knew we'd found our builder.

Design

Cottage Home didn't have to sell us on all the features, and we already knew about and wanted LEED. We were extremely involved in the design process, which took us about a year and a half. Sometimes we'd get overwhelmed with the process between meetings, but then we'd meet again and realize it was the best decision we'd ever made. Brian asked us a number of questions and then roughed out something to see what we thought. He said, "I have thick skin, so just tell me whatever you don't like and we'll change it." But we made very few changes.

Cottage Home's interior designers have a very systematic approach. At our first meeting, they had lots of options laid out. They made it so easy. We picked out carpet from one sample! They anticipated our needs based on the information we gave them. They grasped who we

are. We were surprised when they said we'd meet only once or twice, but that's all it took!

Build

Another house had gone up near us recently, and their builder hadn't communicated with the neighbors at all. It was horrible for the whole neighborhood. We told Brian about how tight the roads are in our community, and how the building project would belong to everyone who lived there. Brian told us that he always introduces himself and Cottage Home to the neighbors at the start of a project. That was the right answer! What builder does that? He even sent letters to our neighbors, and no one has ever done that. The Cottage Home team were good neighbors and good stewards. They didn't want people to contact us if there were issues, so they gave out their contact information. It was pretty amazing.

We spent a lot of time with the workers, bringing them hot cocoa or pizza or taking them out to lunch. Phil knew the name of every person who worked on our house. We were here whenever we could be, sometimes twice a day. Lynn had the never-ending cookie bucket. We were at the site often and got involved with and attached to the people who worked there. We want to have a plaque in our cottage that names each person who worked on it. They built the bones of this house, and we were there when they were doing it. The house wouldn't be there without those guys, and we appreciate them.

Jeremy started taking us on field trips to the facilities that made our counters and other features of our home. They've never done that with a client. They read our enthusiasm through the whole process and responded accordingly. And the contractors sent us a thank you note for allowing them to be involved! We also visited Cottage Home's cabinet shop and met the guys who built all our cabinets. We were really excited about that.

When we were almost done building this house, we got that horrible feeling you get halfway through a vacation. It was a great experience from the start to finish, and we didn't want it to end. It took from February to August to build. We could not have been happier. We didn't believe Brian when he told us the timeline, because it usually takes one and a half or two years.

"The Kennedys genuinely cared about us, and it was great to get to know them. They'd visit and just be so happy about what's going on. Lynn would always be around bringing cookies to the guys. I had some challenges doing detail work in their shower. It was difficult, but once it was done they were so appreciative."

—Karl

"Our community is incredible. One of us will say, 'I'm going down to get the mail—I'll see you in half an hour.' Then they'll bump into neighbors and start talking. We can't help but talk to the neighbors when we're outside. It's a friendly neighborhood with a single lane that promotes a relaxed environment and being outdoors. There are no through streets, so there are no cars going by fast, no traffic, and nowhere else to go. When you're here, you don't want to get in the car."

"They have their process down."

"*You can always trust Cottage Home. We were very particular about some things, but with certain things we just decided to let them do their thing. They never let us down. And get engaged in the process! It's so fulfilling to learn about the inside of your house. We had so much fun, and we'll miss the people.*"

"This was the best decision we've ever made."

> *"We've literally taken thousands of photos of sunsets over the lake. Whenever we think we have enough, there's something different and wonderful."*

Build. Continued.

But Cottage Home stages everything ahead of time, and they made their deadline. It wasn't taxing on the neighborhood like it usually is. One neighbor told us they could tell that the builder was good just because the trucks were clean. Our neighbors love our house, and that's not normal. It's great.

Life on the Lakeshore

We live in our cottage full-time, but we both work for an airline, so we spend several days away from home at a time. We'll be gone for three days, come home, hit the grocery store on the way home, and then try not to leave the house. We don't want to get in the car and go somewhere else. We just want to stay here, and we can hardly wait to get back to the house when we do leave. Phil had to leave recently when it was seventy degrees, sunny, and not a cloud in the sky, and he said to himself, "Why am I leaving? I feel sick, don't I? I should really stay home."

In the spring, summer, and fall we're always outdoors. We see our home as a hub for entertaining, and most of our guests are from across the country. Some of our best friends are from Florida, and we built a room specifically for them. We're casual people and casual entertainers. We might pick a recipe for dinner that everyone can help out with. With Phil's family we do a classic meal where they draw names for a partner and draw a dish, and everyone's involved.

Community

Our community is incredible. Most of the homes have been passed down within families, so the neighborhood has become one big family itself. You know your neighbor's parents and you know their grandkids. One of us will say, "I'm going down to get the mail—I'll see you in half an hour." Then they'll bump into neighbors and start talking. We can't help but talk to the neighbors when we're outside. It's a friendly neighborhood with a single lane that promotes a relaxed environment and being outdoors. There are no through streets, so there are no cars going by fast, no traffic, and nowhere else to go. When you're here, you don't want to get in the car and leave.

We love the Holland, Grand Haven, and Saugatuck area and think it has so much to offer. We get a bunch of pamphlets on local attractions so our guests won't be bored, but they never leave and do anything. People just want to stay at the house! They might go to Holland for dinner or

Saugatuck to walk around, but they can't wait to get back to our cottage.

Legacy

Brian and his team have become good friends. We always joke that we want to work for them one day. Their process is exciting, and they made us feel like rockstars. That includes their contractors, who were so kind and respectful. Some have even come back to visit. We're planning to have a big get-together here for everyone who had a hand in building this house.

We had our twentieth wedding anniversary and were thinking about taking a trip to celebrate. We were looking at Greece and other places abroad, but Lynn finally said, "I don't really want to get on an airplane," and Phil said, "Yes!" We realized that we are fortunate to live in a place where people vacation. We're fortunate that our jobs take us to great places, but there's no place like home. Phil's been all over the world with the navy, but the Southwest Michigan coastline is unique and spectacular. It's incredible, and nobody knows about it! Lynn always says that we have miles of sandy beaches, and people say, "What?" You can be right on the shoreline forever here, and it's pristine. The white sand is squeaky clean and unique compared with other parts of the world. It's way nicer than the rocky beaches on the Wisconsin side. We fly over the shoreline all the time, and our coworkers are wowed by the coastline. "You live THERE?" We love seeing the lakeshore through our guest's eyes, and it keeps us from taking it for granted.

We had the chance to introduce Phil's family to Lake Michigan. They'd never seen it before. Initially, they had no comprehension of what the Big Lake would be like. "This isn't a lake, this is an ocean!" They couldn't believe it. One of our greatest joys is sharing the lakeshore with so many of our friends and family who are not from this area. One friend couldn't believe that there isn't a tide. We spend so much time on the beach with the family.

This Christmas, all of Phil's family members are going to be visiting for a vacation. Usually it's a weeklong summer vacation, and it's bare feet, much food, much sand, and much croquet. We're excited to keep sharing our cottage and the lakeshore with others.

> *"Anybody who's met the Kennedys became friends with them. They came out to see the shop, and they were involved in every part of building because they loved the process. It was fun. They are really nice people. Lynn made us cookies almost every day!"*
>
> *— Josh*

Early in the design process Jeremy said, 'They're trying to put ten pounds of flour in a five pound sack!' Later on, Brian told us that our house has all of the features that Cottage Home has put in all of its other houses combined! That made it a unique and fulfilling experience for the workers."

Kennedy Family Cottage Profile

Lynn was nervous that builders wouldn't be able to keep up with Phil, but that wasn't a problem for Cottage Home. Every detail in the home was very planned and intentional, and as a result it's a really outstanding cottage.

"Phil really knew his stuff. I took great joy in the fact that he understood the things we're so passionate about and could appreciate the quality of our work. When he realized that our competency and passions were in line with what he wanted, it was a great relief for Lynn. We were understanding and implementing everything he was talking about."

— Jeremy

"The Kennedys' house was the most enjoyable house I've ever worked on. It's an awesome home, and it springs from awesome people. Phil and Lynn are one of a kind, and I've worked with thousands of homeowners. With their expertise and graciousness, Brian's creativity, and the team's execution, it turned out amazing."

— Steve

"We wanted a little lookout spot on the top of the house, just something big enough for two seats so we could relax with a glass of wine and watch the sunset. It ended up needing to be bigger because it was required to fit into the roofline. Cottage Home expanded it into one of their signature bunk rooms, with steps between the two sets of two bunks that have storage drawers cleverly tucked underneath. The view is spectacular, with a porthole and old family heirloom incorporated into the design. Best of all, the room is only accessible through a door hidden behind a bookcase!"

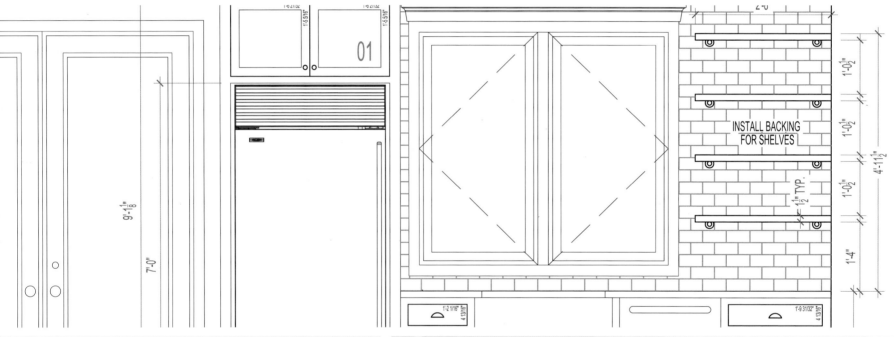

INSTALL BACKING FOR SHELVES

"Cottage Home had never used zip wall before, but they were happy to do it when Phil suggested it, and it saved labor and time and made for a higher-quality wall. We also convinced them to use mineral wool for insulation instead of fiberglass. It's a natural byproduct of iron ore extraction and making steel. It's not affected by water and is a renewable resource. It's also great for soundproofing."

"*Quality was very important to Phil. For example, using 2'x 6' studs instead of 2'x 4' studs for better insulation, radiant heat floors, and high-efficiency, high-quality appliances and windows. Jeremy even found a gutter guard that can actually keep the sand out when it blows in the winter. We'd never seen anything like that before. They even taught Phil some things!*"

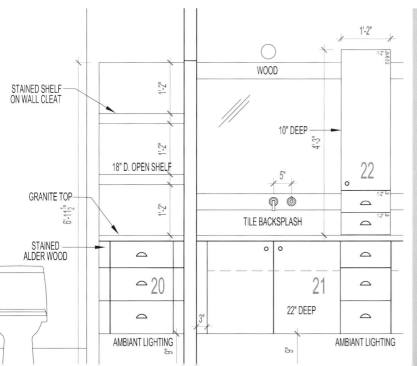

STAINED SHELF
ON WALL CLEAT

WOOD

18" D. OPEN SHELF

10" DEEP

GRANITE TOP

TILE BACKSPLASH

STAINED
ALDER WOOD

20   21

22" DEEP

AMBIANT LIGHTING   AMBIANT LIGHTING

"*It was a really challenging job. We had to run a steel beam through the center of the house to support the loads. There were site challenges, since it was in a critical dune area on the edge of a steep slope. We used some new building components in the project that were complex. It's three stories tall, too, with the chart room up at the top. It was challenging to squeeze that into the attic space and make it functional. But it was a lot of fun.*"

– Doug

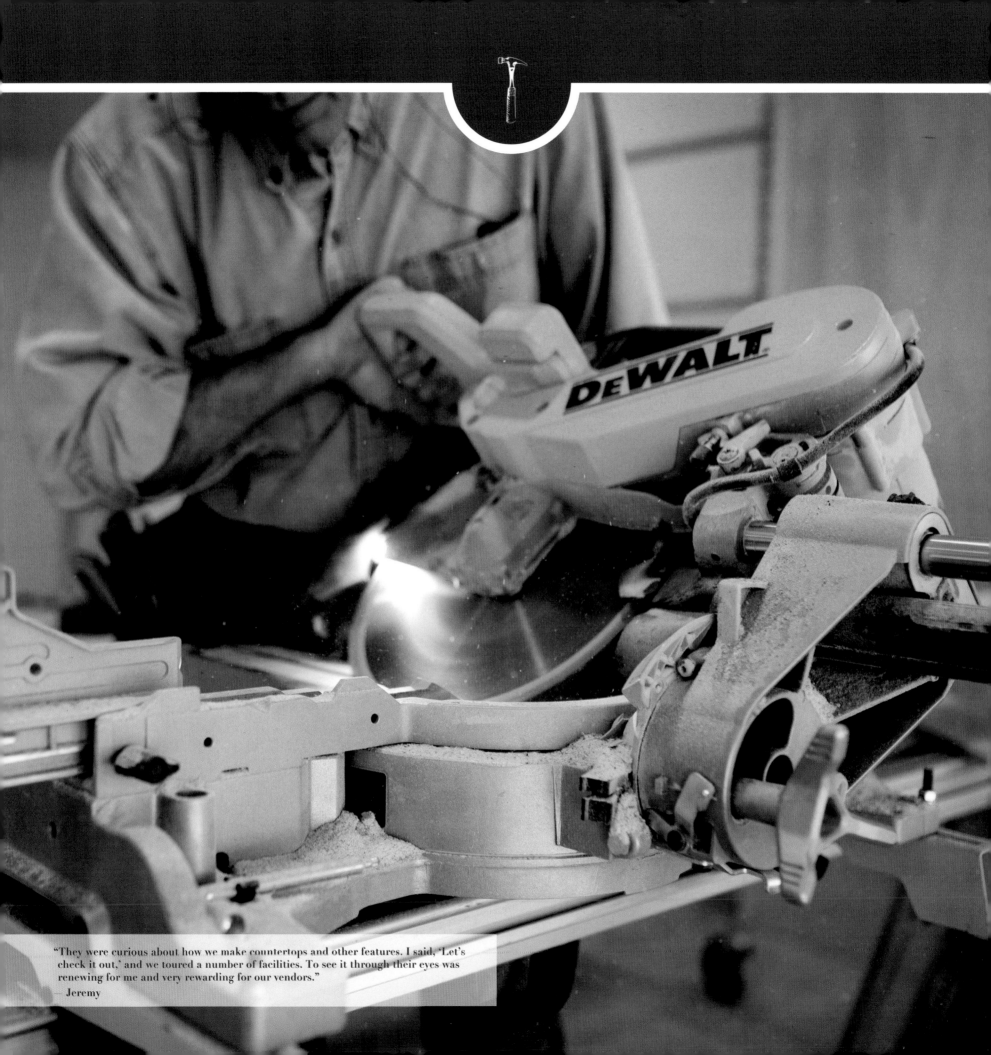

"They were curious about how we make countertops and other features. I said, 'Let's check it out,' and we toured a number of facilities. To see it through their eyes was renewing for me and very rewarding for our vendors."
— Jeremy

"Brian, his people, and their contractors are wonderful. He sets the tone and he doesn't accept anything less than 100% quality. Everybody is free to be the good person they really are."

— Phil and Lynn Kennedy

"We build creative, cool stuff. There's a million ways to build a house, but we feel that we build it the right way. I take a lot of pride in making sure everything's being done the way it should be. Our standards are very high, and quality is always a large factor. And we work very efficiently as a team, and that's what really makes it all come together. I think being organized and having a plan and schedule is extremely important. Then everything clicks together."

— Eric

"There have been many times when the infrastructure wasn't sufficient for the new house, and we facilitated upgrades of the entire system. Then all the electric systems get better in the entire neighborhood. We coordinate with the power company and with the neighbors, whether it's getting Internet to the cottage or taking natural gas down there. Our work enhances the whole community."

— Jeremy

Fireplaces

"Cottage Home built an exact replica of our old fireplace in our new cottage. Barbara loves it, and it's the perfect centerpiece for our dining room and living room area."

— Jack and Barbara Weigle

"We have a lake room with a fireplace. We also have one in the sitting room off our bedroom, which has rocks from our beach in the masonry surround. We love that personal touch that Cottage Home gave us."

— Bob and Bridget Tolpa

"We love hanging out around our wood-burning fireplace, which the team happily installed even though it's somewhat unusual for Cottage Home."

— Guy and Barb Calhoun

Walk-In Pantries

"Initially, Lynn was unsure about tearing down the old house and rebuilding. Then she realized it would mean she could have the walk-in pantry she always wanted, and she was sold. Cottage Home designed a beautiful pantry complete with drawer refrigerators, a sink, and all the storage space you could want. Phil has all of his breakfast supplies right where he needs them by the refrigerator drawers. It's Lynn's happy place."

— Phil and Lynn Kennedy

Farmhouse Tables

Farmhouse tables are a great place for everyone to gather when they're at the lake, whether it's for dinner or for board games. There's always enough seating, and you don't have to be concerned about ruining the rustic top!

Jeremy van Eyk

Vice President and Construction Manager

"Understanding everything that goes into our projects is so important. We get a bit fanatical about documentation, but I always ask myself 'When a client calls in five years to inquire about a paint color, appliance serial number, faucet specs, or what- ever it may be, how quickly can we get them that information?' It makes future care for the home so much easier and more efficient, years after it's built. The same is true for larger projects. When someone decides they'd like to add a bathroom on the third floor, we can get all the plumbing figured out from the office because we have documentation of every pipe, wire, and piece of wood we installed behind the walls. It's better design, more efficient and therefore much less disruptive."

"It's awesome to have such a tangible result of your work that you can see. We take great pride in the homes that we build, and we want to see them withstand the test of time. The lakeshore elements can be tough on a house, but we know which products have proven track records here, and our houses are built to maintain comfort and value for the homeowners for many years to come."

"My role at Cottage Home is to put all the nuts and bolts together and make sure it's all organized. I head up the building process, so my job is to take an incredibly complicated plan and give the client assurance that it's going to be right, it's going to be simple, and it's going to work out. I meet with structural engineers and do a lot of research in order to tell the client how we're going to execute it well, on budget, and on time."

"While much of our work is performed by Cottage Home artisans, we also work with a group of specialized independent contractors to put a house together. Coordinating the schedule so that everyone completes their job on time and on budget takes a lot of communication and planning."

Move-In

"*When construction was finished, we had an open house for all of the workers who built our house. The plumbers, electricians, cabinetmakers, and absolutely everyone else were invited. We thanked everyone and told them that for the first time in our lives, our reality exceeded our dreams. As spooky as that sounds, it's the truth.*"

— Bob and Bridget Tolpa

Move-In

Once the work is done and everything is finished on time and on budget, there's a magical moment when lakeshore homeowners actually move into their new cottages. This first encounter with the cottage becomes just one of the many precious memories they will create on the shores of Lake Michigan. When the big day arrives, we lead clients through a home orientation walkthrough so we can review their new home with them. Cottage Home is also happy to assist clients with move-in.

Many owners use their cottage as a vacation home, so their experience of the house features many smaller move-ins over the years. These clients often come up on the weekends or for more extended vacations in the summer. While summer is the most popular season for cottage dwellers, there's no bad time of year to visit. Some come up to see the fall colors, or even to gather their families together for the winter holidays.

A number of Cottage Home's clients live in their lakeshore cottages full-time, so moving in means moving in for good. This group includes retirees who were commuting back and forth, but have now decided to settle on the lakeshore. Whatever the move-in looks like, it's always an exciting event when someone's lakeshore dream house comes true.

"Cottage Home helped us with move-in, including selecting and bringing in the furniture. Everything was furnished and done on closing day. It was sunny and all the blinds were up when we walked in for the first time. It was another one of those heart-stopping moments. 'This is one of the most beautiful things I've ever seen.' The expansive visibility we have of the lake is amazing."

— John and Lisa Nevins

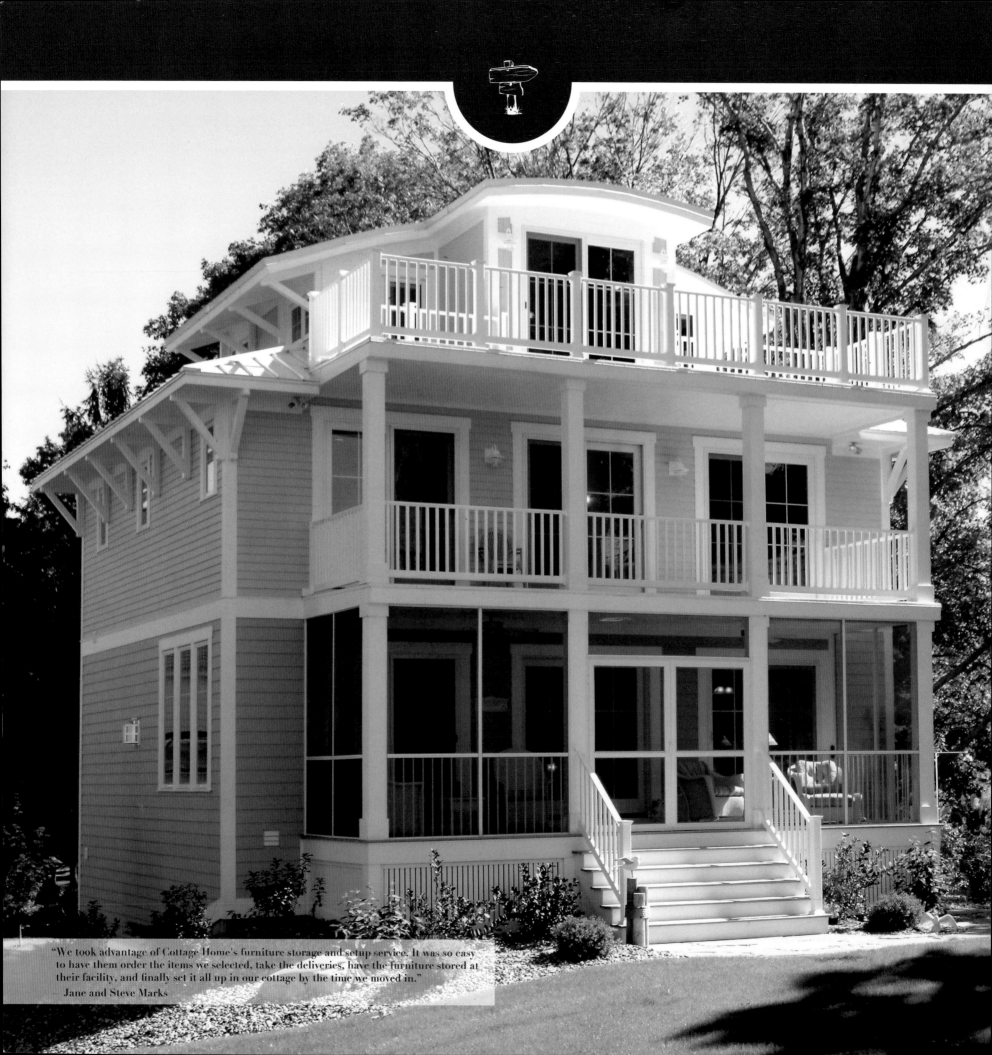

"We took advantage of Cottage Home's furniture storage and setup service. It was so easy to have them order the items we selected, take the deliveries, have the furniture stored at their facility, and finally set it all up in our cottage by the time we moved in."
— Jane and Steve Marks

"For the first time in our lives, our reality exceeded our dreams."

Family Name
The Tolpas

Fun Fact
The cottage isn't just a part of their lifestyle. It IS their lifestyle!

Passions
Sailing, Finding Beach Glass, Local Involvement

Location
South Haven

Bob and Bridget Tolpa's Story

Dream

We used to go to the beach when we were kids, but neither of our families had vacation homes. Our parents would get us up early in the morning, we'd spend the entire day at the beach, and we were exhausted by the end of it. We made some great memories. We both grew up playing on the shores of Lake Michigan, and Bob used to race sailboats on the lake.

We're originally from Northwest Indiana. We spent a lot of our lives in Chicago, moved out to D.C., and then came back to the Chicago area. We're very familiar with Lake Michigan, and it's always been our ambition to have a house on the beach. We wanted to build on the lakeshore for at least twenty years.

Location

As we were driving on the lakeshore We looked for lakefront property in Wisconsin, Illinois, Indiana, and Michigan. When we were still living on the East Coast, Bridget was already looking at lots on Lake Michigan. We knew we were going to move back to Chicago for our jobs, and we were set on buying property and building. Soon, we found a Cottage Home house that looked exactly like what we wanted. Bridget was going to be in the area for business anyway, so she and her mom road tripped up there to take a look. That was when we knew we had found our builder. That was in February, and then in May we went up together for a family wedding. Bridget took the opportunity to show Bob that house and a few other Cottage Home houses, and it was love at first sight. We found a lot in Lakebridge that Cottage Home had developed, and we bought it.

> *"We're living in a lovely house, we have woods in the back, the Big Lake in the front, and we see deer and turkey all the time. Life on the lakeshore really is a dream come true."*

Decision

At the time when we were negotiating the purchase of the lot, Cottage Home required that you start construction within two years. We weren't sure whether we wanted to start construction that soon, so we asked for and got a third year. But we ended up starting construction in less than one year! We were driving up and looking at this lot all the time, and it was a hoot. We apologized to Brian for being so adamant about the third year, and he said it wasn't really a problem. He was pretty sure that we'd start much sooner. He said everyone does.

Design

We walked the property with Brian and then sat down and talked about what we wanted in our house. We're both type A people, so we had come prepared with seven pages of our own notes on what we wanted in the house. Brian wanted to talk about how we live. Do we have big parties? Do we like space by ourselves? Do we both cook? How many people do we usually have over? What kind of views would we want? He would ask us these questions and make little notes and symbols on his notepad. At the end of the meeting he asked us if he had missed anything in our notes, and he hadn't! Everything we wanted was going to be included.

We worked with Cottage Home's staff to pick out all the colors, wood, cabinetry, etc. We also involved our interior decorator. It was a lovely process. The designers got along very well. They had pictures of all the houses they've built for us to reference, and we selected everything in one day, largely based on those references.

Build

We were extremely hands on during the build. The only thing we didn't do was swing a hammer! We came up every single weekend our house was under construction. We brought our plans, two folding beach chairs, our lunch, a tape measure, and an engineer's rule so we could compare the house to the plans. Cottage Home figured out what we were doing after a couple of months, because we'd always send them a complimentary email. Then one weekend we found two adirondack chairs in the spot where we would sit, with a note from Cottage Home. They said they felt sorry that we were sitting on our folding beach chairs and that they thought these would be better. They gave us the chairs to keep, and they're beautiful! They told us much later, after the house was done, that we were the only people who had ever come up every weekend. Our excitement was almost uncontainable. I think friends and family hid from us because we were always talking about the cottage.

Move-In

Before we knew it, the house was done and it was time to move in. We absolutely love the finished product. There are two bedrooms and one bathroom upstairs. Downstairs there's a bedroom, Bob's workshop, and a walkout beach entry area. We have rocks from our beach in the fireplace masonry surround. We just love that personal touch that Cottage Home gives you. The ceiling in our bedroom is entirely bead board. The ceilings in both the screened-in porches were really important to Bob. It looks like you're in something very rustic. Cottage Home put in the ceiling and then the guys put in two by fours as if they were roof rafters. It looks like you're in an outdoor setting. It's great to sit in there; it's a homey, cottagey feel.

When construction was finished, we had an open house for all of the workers who built our house. The plumbers, electricians, cabinetmakers, and absolutely everyone else were invited. We thanked everyone and told them that for the first time in our lives, our reality exceeded our dreams. As spooky as that sounds, it's the truth. I cannot imagine someone building a Cottage Home house and their reality not exceeding their dreams. I don't think it's possible.

> *"It's fun to see the homeowner come in and get excited, because that gets us excited as well."*
>
> —*Dirk*

"It was love at first sight."

"Our excitement was almost uncontainable."

> *"We knew what we wanted, but Brian improved on everything we wanted."*

Aftercare

We've had a few situations where something's gone wrong, and Cottage Home has gone out of their way not only to fix it, but also to share the cost with us. Brian's become a friend, as well as many of his associates. You never feel like someone's not going to answer the phone. They're so attentive, and the after-construction care we've received from them has been phenomenal. And we've never known someone who's built with Cottage Home who didn't have a positive experience. It's just amazing.

Life on the Lakeshore

Our cottage isn't a part of our lifestyle. It IS our lifestyle! And that's exactly what we wanted. We thought we'd come up on the weekends when we could, but we started coming up every single weekend. We've had times when we could come up on a Thursday evening and work from there on Friday. Or we'd do a half day on Friday and drive up. We've had it work out that we could always leave on Monday morning for work. We'd get up early, Bridget would drop Bob off at the train station in Chesterton, and then she would drive herself to work. Rather than it being something we would do when we could, it became something we always did.

Now that we're retired and we live in our cottage full-time, our lifestyle is enviable. Our next-door neighbor says he wants to live like us when he and his wife retire. Bob keeps his sailboat in South Haven's harbor. Sometimes he'll sail past the house and wave, or he'll call Bridget and say, "I'm right on the horizon, can you see me waving?" Of course, he's always too far away and just looks like a speck.

Community

Bob's been retired for three years, and Bridget for four, and now we're really involved locally. South Haven is such a great town. Bridget is chair of public policy for the American Association of University Women, and Bob's a board member for the Michigan Maritime Museum. We're involved in the community for the first time in our lives. Our jobs had never allowed us to get involved in the places we were living before.

Legacy

In summer we have family and friends visit nearly every weekend. We had both of our parents' eightieth birthday parties here. All our siblings, their spouses, and all our parents' grandchildren were here. It's just one of those moments. We couldn't believe we had all these people together. The funny thing is, that totaled seventeen people, and we only have four bedrooms. We had aerobeds all over the place, and no one cared because they were all together on Lake Michigan. It doesn't get any better than that.

Both sides of our family have become almost fanatics about searching for beach glass, something none of us had done before we got this place. A niece we're particularly close with is in the habit of getting up early and saying, "If you see my husband, tell him I'm looking for beach glass." We saw one of our brothers, who is never very emotional about anything, digging around looking for beach glass like a little terrier. Bridget's youngest brother is still working, and he gets up early for his job every day, but we always find him on the beach first thing in the morning, looking for beach glass. He gets up at six to beat everyone else to it. He comes back just bursting with pride at what he found.

At Bridget's mom's eightieth birthday party, she was sitting on the screened-in porch watching her entire family out on the beach looking for beach glass at the same time. They would stop when they passed each other and show each other what they had found. What a hoot! It's one of our favorite memories we've made here.

We're living in a lovely house, we have woods in the back, the Big Lake in the front, and we see deer and turkey all the time. Life on the lakeshore really is a dream come true.

> *Last night we sat outside and watched the sunset with glasses of wine and cheese and crackers. Then we watched the storm come in last night, and today we have fifty-mile-an-hour winds. It looked like a mountain had formed on the lake. It was incredible."*

"The design process was much cooler than we thought it would be. It was a very gentle approach to house design. Rather than grilling us, Brian talked very casually, and he covered everything."

Tolpa Family Cottage Profile

Bob and Bridget literally walked every inch of the beach from the state line to South Haven to find the perfect spot for their vacation home, which is now their retirement residence as well.

"We knew we were going to retire to this house, so there were certain things that we wanted. We have two full bathrooms on the main floor so we wouldn't have to share. We have a sitting room off our bedroom with a fireplace. Everything we need is on the main floor."

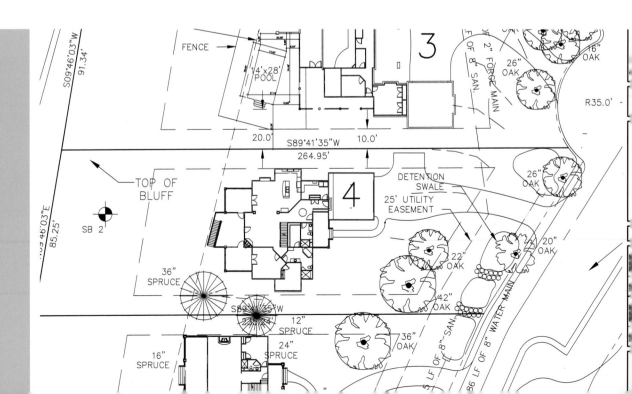

"We really like the beach feeling of Cottage Home's houses. We love river rock, transoms wherever you can get them, and bead board. We like rooms that are not too small and not too big, rooms that you can do multiple things in."

"Enjoy the process. Don't worry, it'll be perfect. Our only slight regret is that we didn't take a deep breath and watch it unfold. We didn't really savor it because we were so cranked up about it, and we didn't need to be."

The Tolpas' Compass Rose

"Bob is a sailor, so he asked Cottage Home to put a compass rose medallion in the wood floor of our entryway. He even had it set by GPS to make sure the north is true."

Beach and Pool Toy Storage

Paddle boards, kayaks, fishing gear, pool and beach toys, and all the accessories that go with them—having fun in the sun involves a lot of gear! Cottage Home clients keep it all together with a variety of toy storage structures.

"I've helped Ross numerous times with taking out the Iaderosa's pool furniture and putting it back in. That is my favorite house that we've built, the ultimate party house for a big group. And of course, whenever we go over there to put their pool furniture in or out, it's definitely not the nicest day of the year! But we do it so that when it is nice, they can be there and enjoy it."

– Eric

"We have a storage room for all our toys right down by the pool area. It was nice to have that figured out for us."
– John and Lisa Nevins

Windows

"We're not actually on the lakeshore, so it was important to us to maximize the view. We kept adding windows, and we're glad that we did. Our new house is also higher than the old one, making for a much wider arc of views. Brian rotated the house to improve the views. He was incredible at figuring out what to do. He'd be quiet for a meeting while we were discussing it with the rest of the staff, and then once we'd talked ourselves through it, he'd draw out exactly what we wanted! It was pretty amazing."

— Phil and Lynn Kennedy

"We told Brian that when we walked into our house, we wanted to see the thing that drew us here in the first place: the Big Lake. And from our screened-in porch, living/family room, and even our bedroom, we get to see this vast expanse of Lake Michigan. It's beautiful."

— *John and Lisa Nevins*

"The view from our cottage just grabs you right away. Every room has a view of the lake."

— *Guy and Barb Calhoun*

"Brian told us that we would want as many windows as we could get. And that wasn't just for ourselves, he said—we might want to sell the house eventually, and buyers would want to be able to turn the rooms into something else. And he was absolutely right."

— *Bob and Bridget Tolpa*

Dirk Bronsink

Site Management and Carpentry

"My passion, and Cottage Home's passion, is customer service and satisfaction, making sure that the client's needs and wants are met. Whether it's the design process, the build process, or afterwards, I'm always asking what I can do on a daily basis to make their lives easier. Also, I just love seeing a job come together from beginning to completion. The teamwork and all the details that a hundred different people are thinking about create an incredible house in the end."

"Wherever things need to be done, I go do it. That includes a lot in the rough-in and trim stages. I'm moving into site management as time goes on. Basically, I smooth out the wrinkles in the process wherever something's needed."

Life on the Lakeshore

"*Our cottage isn't a part of our lifestyle. It IS our lifestyle! And that's exactly what we wanted. We thought we'd come up on the weekends when we could, but we started coming up every single weekend. And now that we're retired and we live in our cottage full time, our lifestyle is enviable.*"

— Bob and Bridget Tolpa

Life on the Lakeshore

Finally, what the whole lakeshore story has been building up to: life on Lake Michigan. Once they've settled in, Cottage Home's clients take full advantage of their homes and the beach. Everyone lives a busy life, but the lakeshore is a place where you can escape. When you're on the beach, you can simply relax and enjoy the moments.

The lakeshore is a place for spending time with family and friends, making memories that you'll treasure for years to come. It's a place for endless outdoor activities: swimming, kayaking, paddle boarding, boating, sailing, fishing, relaxing on the beach, walking up and down the shore, searching for beach glass, playing games in the back yard—the list goes on and on. Lakeshore cottages are also homes to be enjoyed for their own sake.

Weekend or weeklong vacations, family reunions, parties with friends old and new, and peaceful, joyful day-to-day living—however our clients choose to live on the lakeshore, they are living a dream come true.

"We live a really hectic lifestyle, and we don't get to spend a lot of time together most days. We divide and conquer, rushing the kids around. But our cottage has become the place where we all go to take a deep breath and hang out together. It's the only place where we actually sit around the table and eat together, play baseball and football, kayak, and paddle board. We were worried that we wouldn't be able to spend time as a family while the kids were growing up, but our cottage has made that possible."

— Jon and Sherri Newpol

"The lakeshore lifestyle allows family and friends to come together. It gives them a reason to spend time together and do things that are out of the ordinary."
— Wendy

"A lot of the time I take living in Southwest Michigan for granted. The lakeshore and all the nature are just amazing. The shoreline from South Haven through Holland is all truly incredible. That's what draws other people to this area. It's a very inviting and welcoming place."
— Steve

"I've lived in West Michigan my whole life, and it's all been purposeful. I love the lakeshore, and I just can't imagine a better place to live and raise our family. It's awesome. Our kids love growing up at the beach. We just love the lakeshore and the lifestyle it offers. I feel like I can tell if I'm not around water!"
Stephanie

"Cottage Home stands by their houses. If we had any issues, they were there to take care of things. It was a great experience."

Family Name

The Sanfords

Features

Three Balconies, Tilt-Up
Window, Views of the
Lake and River

Passions

The National Blueberry
Festival, Relaxed Living

Location

South Haven

Amy and Todd Sanford's Story

Dream

We wanted a vacation home so we could get away from it all. We live in Southwest Michigan near Kalamazoo, so we were familiar with both Lake Michigan and the nearby inland lakes. However, we aren't boaters, so we weren't particularly attracted to the smaller lakes. Amy's family had a place on Lake Michigan up in Muskegon, so she'd had some experience with the lakeshore. We both loved Lake Michigan's beaches and the things you could do there—walking the beach, sitting on the beach, relaxing, warm breezes, great sunsets, and enjoying the beauty and uniqueness of the Big Lake.

Location and Decision

We weren't really thinking seriously about looking for a home on the lakeshore—it kind of just happened. We were at a bed and breakfast in Douglas and were just walking around when we saw a couple of Cottage Home houses for sale. We thought, "This is interesting." We had been talking about looking for a vacation property for a long time, but we hadn't decided where, except that a property on an inland lake wouldn't meet our needs. Right then and there, we decided that maybe the Lake Michigan beach would be a better location.

We were attracted to the style of Cottage Home's houses, especially the colors, porches, wood floors, and porthole windows. It all started from there. After looking at the houses we went on Cottage Home's website and decided to take another look, this time at some of their homes in Douglas and South Haven.

"This being our first build, we relied heavily on the team's expertise to do what they would do if it were their own home, and we were not disappointed."

Design

This was our first build, and it was a really easy process for us even though we had no experience. We had purchased a postage stamp size lot in South Haven, so we knew we had limitations. We just told the Cottage Home team how many bedrooms we wanted, informed them of certain other features that were important to us, and mentioned that we wanted as many decks and porches as we could get to create extra space. Then the team presented us with a design that went up as high as we could in order to maximize space. We think of it as a mini skyscraper, actually.

Cottage Home absolutely took our needs into account. We told them what we needed to have, and from there it was about what else could be done given our limitations. We knew it would be challenging to design the structure that would be required to support a tall home with narrow stairs and things of that nature. But they did a wonderful job maximizing the space. We liked their recommendations, so we didn't make a lot of changes to the layout they proposed.

Cottage Home helped us pick out all the appliances, and they helped us with design and color schemes. They were thorough from start to finish. And the timing was unbelievable! They tore down the existing house around Thanksgiving, and we got the keys before tax filing time in April. There were no delays. It took four months from start to finish. It was amazing.

Build and Move-In

Amy was involved with all the design details, like choosing colors and styles. However, we weren't terribly involved when it came time to build the cottage. We'd visit periodically to check things out, but we were mostly hands-off except when called upon to make a decision. We would provide feedback, but Cottage Home did the lion's share of the work and made some decisions for us based on their experience that

we knew only they could make. This being our first build, we relied heavily on the team's expertise to do what they would do if it were their own home, and we were not disappointed.

Once we moved in, we got really excited about our unique Cottage Home. First of all, the way the house was situated is fantastic. On one side we have a wonderful view of Lake Michigan, and on the other side we can see the Black River. You can see water from literally every window of our house. We think that's really unique, and we always talk to people about it.

Space could have been an issue, but our decks give us extra seating outdoors. We have a small front porch and three decks on the back—one is a screened-in porch, one's a master bedroom deck, and the third is a robin's nest, for lack of better term, that gives you magnificent views of Lake Michigan. The decks are pretty special on this house. We absolutely love our screened-in porch. We also have a porthole window and a tilt-up window operated by a pulley system, which is awesome. It's right in our kitchen and looks out onto the porch. That's a really special feature to everyone who sees it.

Life on the Lakeshore

Todd owns a business, and it's exceptionally busy all the time. We were after any place where we could find some respite without a lot of drive time, and that's what our cottage gives us. We love to take walks on the beach for exercise and to collect beach glass. The kids especially enjoyed that when they were young. It was a family thing to do, and the beach is so close and convenient out our back yard. We love to enjoy the screened-in porch at night by candlelight with a glass of wine. We have a lot of memories of nice, relaxing moments like that.

It's a small house on a small lot, but there is still a lot of room inside and on the decks. Brian and his team designed it so we would never want for living space or beds. We've always wanted it to be a nice place to enjoy, not a show home with fine, expensive furnishings. A lot of it's just painted trim and oak floors with medium gray carpets, but the views are just spectacular, and that's what we really wanted. We're glad that we can enjoy and experience the house without worrying about it being a home for the rich and famous, so to speak. It's very comfortable, and that's the way we like it.

"You can't find a better place to watch the South Haven fireworks than the Sanfords' house."

—Eric

"It was amazing."

"We have a lot of memories
of nice, relaxing moments."

> *"It's nice to have those little shops, ice cream parlors, and small town events for Fourth of July and that sort of thing. It brings you back to a different time, like it's fifty years ago. It's like time stands still in these little towns."*

Community

This shore of Lake Michigan has spectacular sand, as good or better as anywhere else in the world. And it's particularly beautiful because you can watch the sun setting over the lake. Red sunsets on the beach are spectacular. Everyone in South Haven comes out to watch the sun go down, and everybody claps if it's a particularly nice sunset. That's something that we'll always remember, no matter where we are down the road. We don't know of any other place where you can get that. You can't experience that on an inland lake or really anywhere else. And the communities up and down the lakeshore, including South Haven, have a wonderful small town feel. It's nice to have those little shops, ice cream parlors, and small town events for Fourth of July and that sort of thing. It brings you back to a different time, like it's fifty years ago. It's like time stands still in these little towns. And we always look forward to the Blueberry Festival in South Haven and having family out for that.

Legacy

Our kids have had just as much fun with the cottage as we have. They enjoy inviting their friends out and sharing the beach and home with them. We've done a fair amount of entertaining with family at the house. On important holiday weekends we try to have people out and enjoy it. We were at our cottage for Thanksgiving one year, and we actually had dinner outside on the patio because it happened to be a beautiful, warm day.

Working with Cottage Home was wonderful, and our cottage in South Haven has been the perfect place for us to get away. In our experience, Cottage Home is a conscientious, high-quality builder that we would highly recommend, and that's why we're going to build with them again. We recently purchased a new lot in Fennville with direct access to Lake Michigan, and we plan to build again with Cottage Home in a year or two. Brian and his team were incredibly helpful when we were picking out the property, showing us lots of options up and down the lakeshore and telling us what can and can't be done in their eyes. We've learned that each site on the lakeshore has its own set of opportunities and challenges, and that you need somebody who's highly experienced and can help you pick out the right lot. It's incredibly valuable to have an advisor with that kind of knowledge and expertise.

The Cottage Home team is very connected in all areas of the lakeshore,

and that helped us make a good decision and be conscientious toward our new neighbors. We wanted to clear the lot we just bought, since it was overrun with trees and brush. Brian was in agreement because he said it would also improve the neighbors' views. Sure enough, both of our neighbors in Fennville were very pleased. Now we have a good relationship with them before we've even set one foot out on the property to enjoy it. We're making friends, not creating animosity or challenges. It gives us peace of mind to know that Cottage Home is on our side as we get ready to embark on another lakeshore journey.

> *"Todd and Amy have had us back to do several projects over the years, and recently they contacted us when they started thinking of moving from their city lot to a private beach lot. They asked me what I recommended, and I shared a site Cottage Home was interested in. They put an offer in, and the seller just took it! They were happy that the Sanfords were working with us, since they respected the work we'd already done in the area. Now, ten years after the original project, we're designing them a new house."*
>
> *—Brian*

"We love to enjoy the screened-in porch at night by candlelight with a glass of wine."

Sanford Family Cottage Profile

Todd and Amy built this cottage in the Harbor District of South Haven. It's intended to be a place for their family to get away. More recently, they purchased direct lakefront property in Fennville to build on again, this time in a more serene location.

"We also have a porthole window and a tilt-up window operated by a pulley system, which is awesome. It's right in our kitchen and looks out onto the porch. That's a really special feature to everyone who sees it."

"Our decks give us extra seating outdoors. We have a small front porch and three decks on the back—one is a screened-in porch, one's a master bedroom deck, and the third is a robin's nest, for lack of better term, that gives you magnificent views of Lake Michigan. The decks are pretty special on this house."

"The way the house was situated is fantastic. On one side we have a wonderful view of Lake Michigan, and on the other side we can see the Black River. You can see water from literally every window of our house."

Local Festivals

Local festivals are one of the true delights of the lakeshore communities. Captivating natives and visitors alike, these celebrations bustle with energy without being too crowded or chaotic. Each year, South Haven has HarborFest, the Classic Wooden Boat Show, the Art Fair, the National Blueberry Festival, and the IceBreaker Festival. Holland has its world-famous Tulip Time, plus an annual Civil War muster in the fall. Saugatuck and Douglas celebrate the Jazz Festival, the Taste of Saugatuck food festival, the Gallery Stroll, and the Halloween Festival. And this is only the tip of the iceberg. Overall, Southwest Michigan's local festivals provide food, fun, and enough variety to please the whole family.

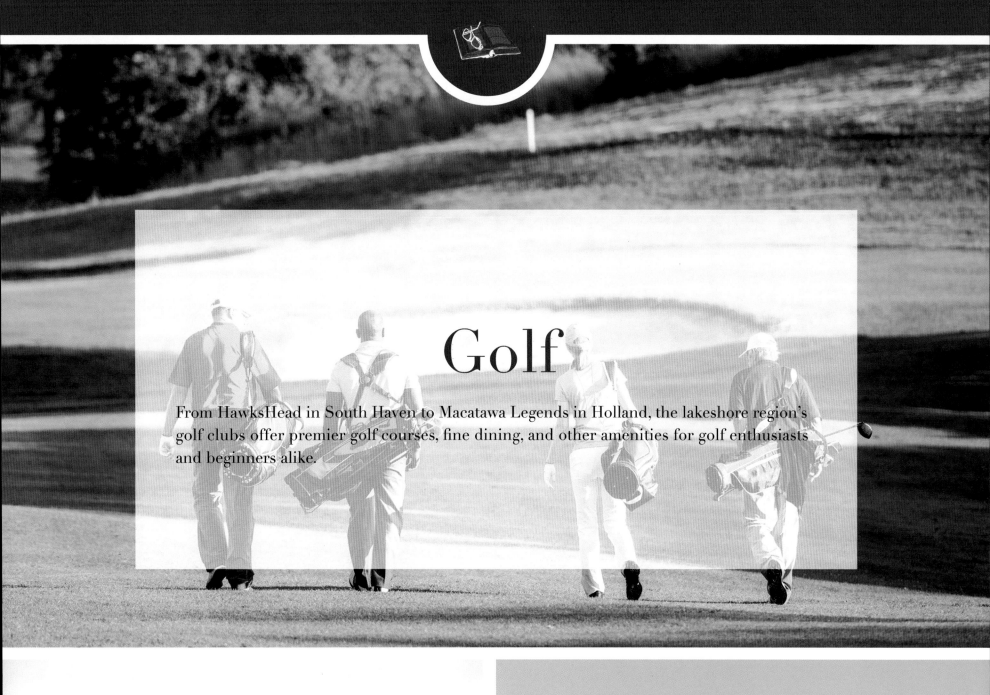

Golf

From HawksHead in South Haven to Macatawa Legends in Holland, the lakeshore region's golf clubs offer premier golf courses, fine dining, and other amenities for golf enthusiasts and beginners alike.

"When Steve retires, we might move up here full-time, or maybe half-time. He loves to play golf and be active outside, and the lakeshore has so many opportunities."

— Jane and Steve Marks

Outdoor Showers

After a day at the beach, it feels great to rinse off the sand before heading inside. Cottage Home makes this possible with outdoor showers. They're a key feature for keeping the inside of the cottage clean, and for keeping guests happy.

"*We have an outdoor shower where people can clean off after being at the beach or in the pool.*"

— *John and Lisa Nevins*

The Lakeshore Lifestyle

"The Cottage Home team likes to have fun. Especially in the summer we'll get out and do things together on the lakeshore. One of the guys has a boat, so sometimes we go out fishing together."

— Dirk

"I've lived in West Michigan my whole life, and it's all been purposeful. I love the lakeshore, and I just can't imagine a better place to live and raise our family. It's awesome. Our kids love growing up at the beach. We just love the lakeshore and the lifestyle it offers. I feel like I can tell if I'm not around water!"

— Stephanie

"The lakeshore lifestyle allows family and friends to come together. It gives them a reason to spend time together and do things that are out of the ordinary."

— Wendy

"The lakeshore and all the nature are just amazing. The shoreline from South Haven through Holland is all truly incredible. That's what draws other people to this area. It's a very inviting and welcoming place."

— Steve

"The community and the people here on the lakeshore are just so easy-going. You can't get too upset about the little things in life when there's so much you can enjoy, both on and off the lake. This area has a 'relax and enjoy life' tone that you don't find in other places."

— Justin

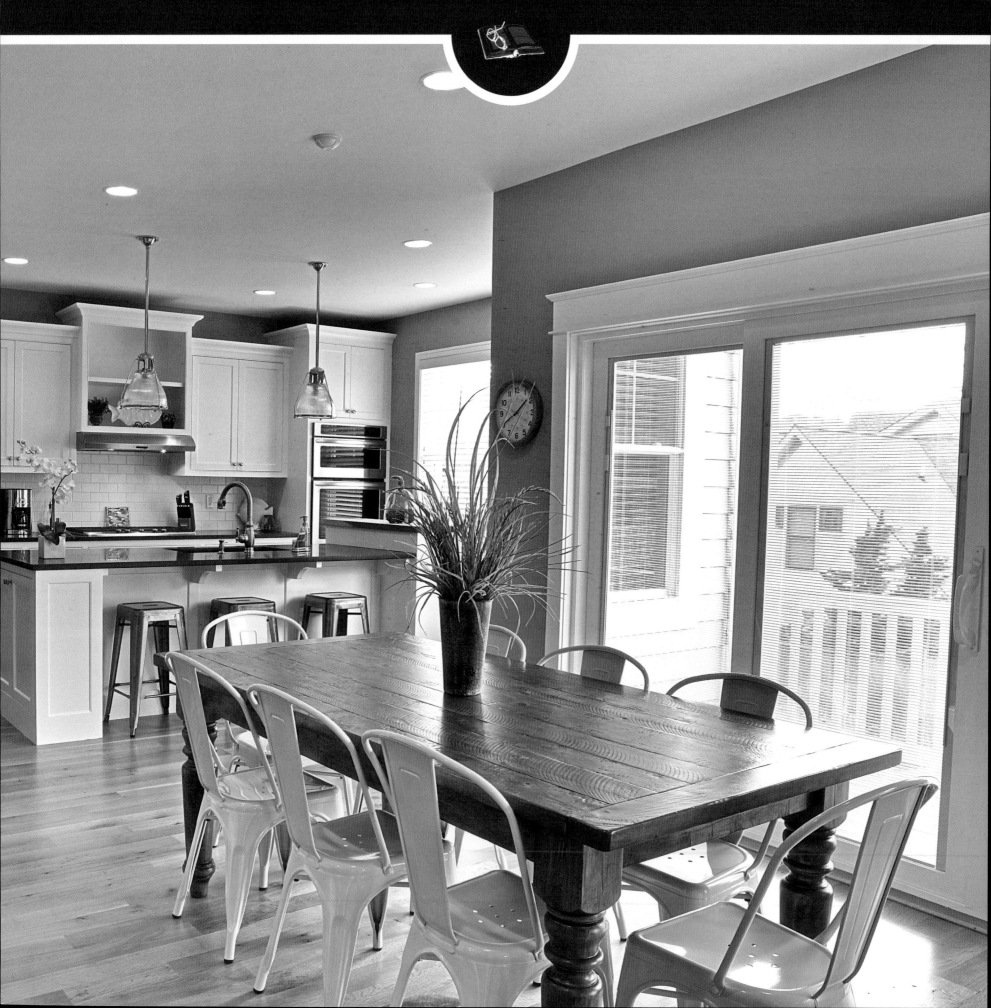

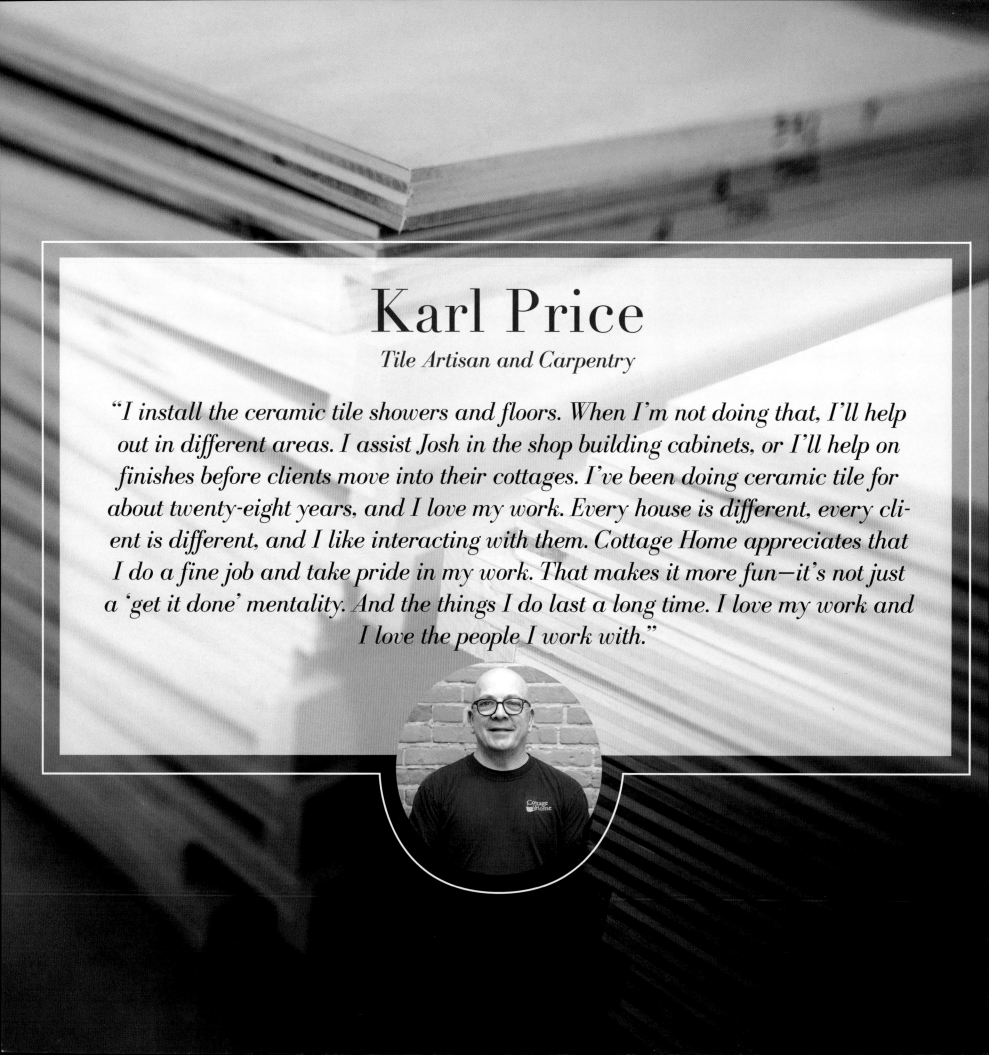

Karl Price

Tile Artisan and Carpentry

"I install the ceramic tile showers and floors. When I'm not doing that, I'll help out in different areas. I assist Josh in the shop building cabinets, or I'll help on finishes before clients move into their cottages. I've been doing ceramic tile for about twenty-eight years, and I love my work. Every house is different, every client is different, and I like interacting with them. Cottage Home appreciates that I do a fine job and take pride in my work. That makes it more fun—it's not just a 'get it done' mentality. And the things I do last a long time. I love my work and I love the people I work with."

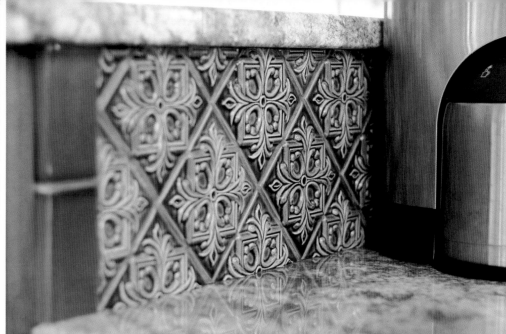

"I live on a little hobby farm about fifteen miles from the lake. I'm not right on Lake Michigan. but I like to go hiking at Saugatuck Dunes State Park. Southwest Michigan is a place that really values family and faith, and I've always been happy to live here. There are relaxing and fun things to do without it being too busy."

esign. Buil
fun from the S

○ *Aftercare*

"*We've had a few situations where something's gone wrong, and Cottage Home has gone out of their way not only to fix it, but also to share the cost with us. The team has become our friends. You never feel like someone's not going to answer the phone. They're so attentive, and the after-construction care we've received from them has been phenomenal.*"

— *Bob and Bridget Tolpa*

⊙ Aftercare

Cottage Home doesn't disappear once our clients move into their new lakeshore cottage. We want to maintain our relationship far into the future, so we make ourselves available to help out with any needs that may arise. Our warranty and cottage watch programs ensure that clients have someone they can rely on to help them maintain their dream home.

The Cottage Home team often checks in on cottages to make sure that everything is as it should be. This includes performing routine maintenance as well as preparing the cottage for the client's visits. Our attentiveness means that when issues do arise, we catch them early and resolve them before they become major problems. Sometimes we even run errands or do odd jobs for clients to help facilitate the perfect lakeshore experience. That could mean anything from hanging a new piece of art to setting up furniture or receiving a Christmas gift someone ships to their cottage.

Nothing should detract from a client's enjoyment of their Lake Michigan cottage. Cottage Home's aftercare services make sure that their lakeshore story remains a happy one.

"One time we needed to do something in a wall, but we didn't know what was behind it. Jeremy told us that Cottage Home knew exactly what was behind the wall. It turns out that they take pictures of every single wall at every single stage of construction so if anything ever comes up, they can basically look at an X-ray of the home. If you want to know where an electrical wire goes, everything is documented and accessible. We couldn't believe their process."

— Anthony and Jenny Iaderosa

"Our clients from out of state don't want to think about their place when they're not here. I tell them, 'Let us worry about the house so that you can enjoy your Cottage Home. You don't have to be concerned about the house; your concern is having fun.'"

— Ross

"*I like to think about the houses we build as having a greater purpose. We're helping people create memories and live a lifestyle that's all about family and friends. When I'm helping to maintain the cottage, that contributes to their enjoyment of the home and makes life easier for them.*"

— Stephanie

"I get early morning and late night phone calls. I find some funny critters that get into cottages sometimes. I've walked into cottages where people forgot to turn the heat on, and that caused serious water damage. They weren't on our cottage watch program at the time, but they sure are now!"

Ross

The Cottage Watch Program

"Since moving in, we've been very impressed by how much Cottage Home cares for their product. Their cottage watch program is fantastic. It's so nice to have someone here once a month to check in. The team's commitment to the house is amazing, and their commitment to the homeowner is outstanding."

— Jane and Steve Marks

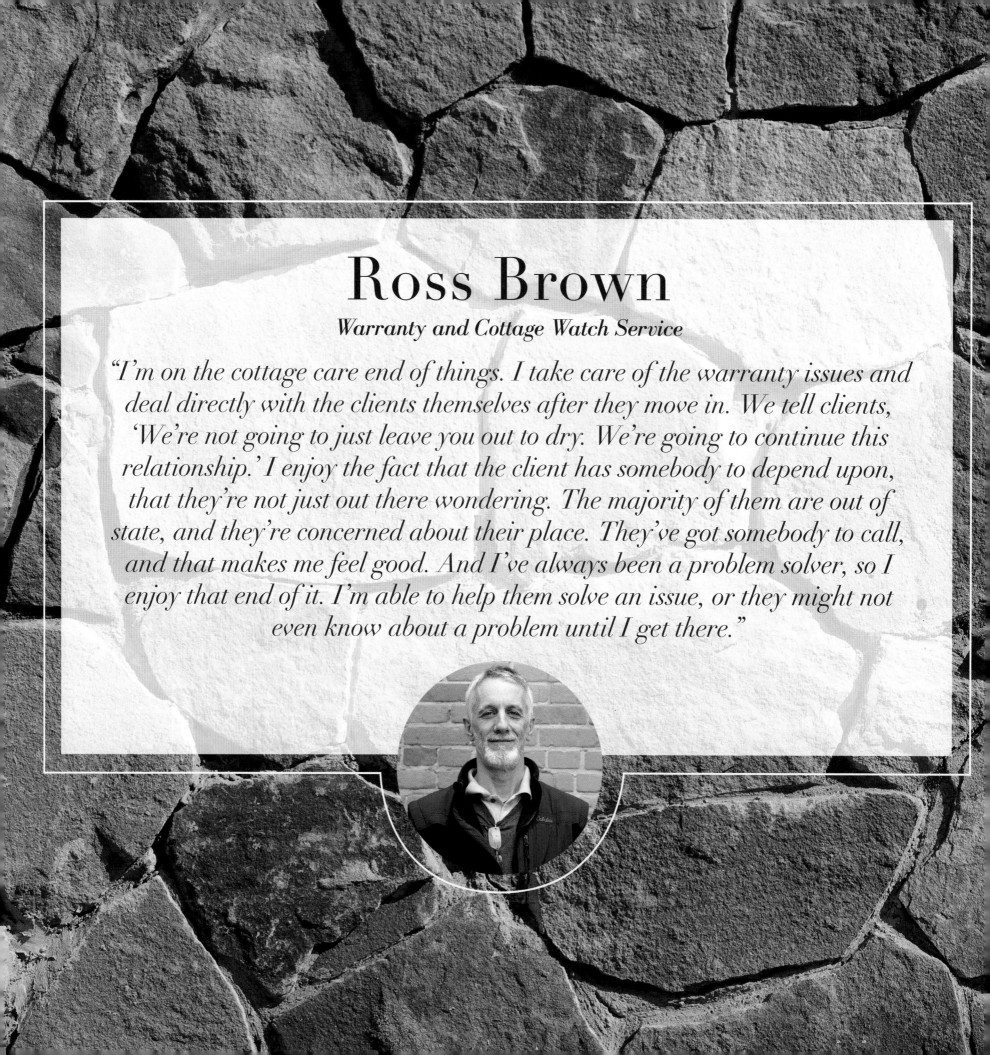

Ross Brown

Warranty and Cottage Watch Service

"I'm on the cottage care end of things. I take care of the warranty issues and deal directly with the clients themselves after they move in. We tell clients, 'We're not going to just leave you out to dry. We're going to continue this relationship.' I enjoy the fact that the client has somebody to depend upon, that they're not just out there wondering. The majority of them are out of state, and they're concerned about their place. They've got somebody to call, and that makes me feel good. And I've always been a problem solver, so I enjoy that end of it. I'm able to help them solve an issue, or they might not even know about a problem until I get there."

Find. Design. Build.
Lakeshore living fun from the start.

"We do a cottage watch program on many of our houses. It's my job to go in once a month, in some cases once a week, to turn the water on, make sure everything's good, the heat's on, a tree hasn't fallen through a window, stuff like that. It makes me feel good, and it gives the client peace of mind to know that they've got somebody to call on. And I enjoy the relationship that I have with many of our clients."

"We're a trusted advisor to our clients. We're someone that they feel comfortable calling if they have an issue. We know where every stud and pipe is, and they know that we'll carry through with quality and care. We really care about our end product, and we're always trying to improve our process."

— Stephanie

"We've said so many times over the year, when we've needed something done at our other house, 'Why can't there be someone like Cottage Home here?'"

— Anthony and Jenny Iaderosa

"I've helped Ross numerous times with taking out the Iaderosa's pool furniture and putting it back in. That is my favorite house that we've ever built, the ultimate party house for a big group. And of course, whenever we go over there to put their pool furniture in or out, it's definitely not the nicest day of the year! But we do it so that when it is nice, they can be there to enjoy it."

— Eric

"When we say 'clients for life,' we mean it. It's real. It's so important to continue a relationship with the homeowners. We have a real commitment to making things work no matter what."

— Steve

Caring for Cottages

"When we give the homeowner a date, we keep to that date. Sometimes that means putting in some extra hours. And we get it done right, in a way that will make the client happy. And we really take care of people afterwards, too. Whenever I talk to people afterward, they're so grateful. It's pretty cool to see them so happy."

— Karl

"*A few weekends ago we received a call from Ross, who had noticed that a tree was down in the road and was blocking the way to our cottage. We called to ask if Cottage Home could do something about it, and they said, "Sure!" A bit later, we went outside and found Ross cutting away at the tree! He totally ruined his chainsaw, but he got it out of the way so our guests could get through.*"

— *Jane and Steve Marks*

"The house was almost finished when we realized that it had no bathtubs, only showers. We mentioned it to the Cottage Home team, and they agreed that it was a good point. They were really fair about the oversight, charging us for the tub itself but not the labor. They just figured out where they could fit it in and did it without any kind of argument, explanation, or tension."

— John and Lisa Nevins

Problem Solving

"Years after we finished the Iaderosas' house, I got a call from Jenny, and she was in tears. An icemaker had malfunctioned and had been leaking for well over a month, and it completely buckled the beautiful wooden floor in their kitchen. The custom cabinets were wrecked. Their kitchen was a complete mess. The ceiling had collapsed into the bedroom below and soaked the carpet. It was horrific. She was asking me whether this could ever look right again. She was devastated. I went out right away to check it out. I knew that wood floor, and I knew we could get the exact same flooring. I told her we'd blend it in perfectly. I assured her that we could take care of everything and make it right again. It was a big project, but it turned out like nothing had ever happened. We put it all back together."

— Jeremy

Four Seasons of Fun

"There's nothing better than watching a sunset over Lake Michigan on a beautiful summer evening. It's amazing to be out paddling when the water is still and calm, but it's also wonderful to be inside when the wind is howling and the waves are crashing on the shore. Sometimes the icebergs are just off shore, and the waves look like their twenty feet high smashing against them. It's awe-inspiring. You can get out on snowshoes or skis in the winter. It's a great experience."

— Brian

"In the summer the scenery brings together sunshine and water, and it's very inviting and enjoyable. In fact, all four seasons are magnificent on the lake, especially the fall with all its colors."

— Guy and Barb Calhoun

Every year we leave on December 26 and stay through New Year's. We invite friends and their families, and our kids bring friends. It's become a winter tradition. There's a little ski resort in Otsego called Bittersweet, and we've probably taught twenty of our kids' friends how to ski there. It's been great for my kids and their friends. It's a great memory. I like that this ski resort is small, friendly, and easy.."

— Anthony and Jenny Iaderosa

"Our house is a platinum LEED home. We didn't know much about that going in, but we thought it was pretty cool once Cottage Home talked to us about it. Our cottage is sustainable. We're recycling and using some geothermal energy. The house has things built into the design that keep heat from being released. It's become important to us."

— *John and Lisa Nevins*

"Cottage Home gave us our first experience with someone who builds LEED homes, as our cottage was the first LEED home in South Haven. The design includes a tank out back that collects rainwater to irrigate the yard. The house is airtight and energy efficient, and all the materials came from within a 500-mile radius."

— Guy and Barb Calhoun

LEED Certification

Cottage Home cares about the environment, and that's why we're a leader in LEED certification on the lakeshore. Leadership in Energy and Environmental Design (LEED) is a green building certification developed by the U.S. Green Building Council. Its goal is to rate the design, construction, operation, and maintenance of buildings, including homes, on environmental responsibility and efficient use of resources. Cottage Home's houses consistently earn a platinum rating, the highest possible LEED certification. We are committed to meeting LEED standards and making the lakeshore environment cleaner and greener for everyone.

"We're stewards of the land. We always consider what's appropriate for the environment."

— Jeremy

"I like fixing the land, resolving the issues. Everything we come across is messed up. Everything's been touched or used or abused, and it's in our company's ethic to fix it and leave it clean, beautiful, and better than it was, both for the environment and for the owners."

— Brian

"We like the fact that they focus on LEED design along the lakeshore. Cottage Home is environmentally conscious and mindful of those around you, and that's really appealing to us."

— Amy and Todd Sanford

Caring for the Environment

Lakeshore properties are not always perfect at first. Most are affected to some extent by erosion and other environmental issues. But the beauty of Lake Michigan's beaches can be restored with the proper skill and effort. Cottage Home is committed to protecting the environment in the way it builds on the lakeshore. This includes LEED, which ensures that the cottage itself is green, and reshaping bluffs and beaches to make them more natural. All this effort enhances our clients' enjoyment of their lakeshore story.

Stephanie Bauman

Client Services and Marketing

"I have the fun job of helping with Cottage Home's marketing, which includes a variety of tasks such as designing content for our newsletters and planning our annual summer events. In more recent years I've also been helping with our warranty service and the cottage watch program as that has grown. Clients from out of state wanted peace of mind, and we're the ones in the area that they trust, since we've built that relationship with them. They were asking us for assistance in keeping an eye on the house, so we gladly put together this program, and it's been great."

"I often get calls from clients years after their home is built. They want to do some sort of special project or improvement. Since we have such great documentation on how the house was built, these projects are fun and often relatively straightforward. I really enjoy reconnecting with past clients in this way."

"Cottage Home has been such a great fit for me. I feel that we're so much more than a home design/ build company, and it's fun to be a part of that greater purpose of investing in our lakeshore community. Our company culture is outstanding, and I'm grateful to be a part of it."

Find. Design. Build.
Lakeshore living fun from the start.

"We were concerned about what might break, how much it would cost to fix, and how big of a deal it would be. Never having owned a home on Lake Michigan, we didn't understand until a few months in how strong the storms can be. But Cottage Home has years of experience and knows what materials work in such harsh weather. Our cottage stands up against heavy rains, strong winds, ice, and frigid temperatures. It's been a huge advantage so far, and we've had no problems."

— *John and Lisa Nevins*

Sustainability on the Lakeshore

"We build houses that are sustainable and lasting. The weather can be pretty harsh on a house on the lakeshore, but we build them so they're easy to maintain and live in. We also provide aftercare services so you can retain the value of your investment without going to all the trouble yourself."

— Brian

Community

"The communities up and down the lakeshore have a wonderful small town feel. It's nice to have those little shops, ice cream parlors, and small town events for Fourth of July and that sort of thing. It brings you back to a different time, like it's fifty years ago. It's like time stands still in these little towns."

— Amy and Todd Sanford

⚓ Community

People build cottages on the Lake Michigan shoreline because it's a cool place to live. There are the cottages and private beaches, of course, but that's not all.

Dotting the lakeshore are communities like South Haven, Saugatuck, Holland, and others that add to the region's appeal. These small towns pack a big punch in terms of entertainment, culture, and the arts. There's a texture and rhythm to life in these lakeshore towns that is utterly unique. They're charming, welcoming, friendly places to visit for a meal, a festival, or just a leisurely stroll. The pace of life is slow and relaxing here, meaning you can just unwind and enjoy.

After a while, our clients start to get to know their neighbors. Many lakeshore neighborhoods are generational communities, with cottages being passed down from parents to children. This results in tight-knit communities where people enjoy each other's company and build strong friendships. Owners of Cottage Homes find out that they haven't just gained their dream home—they've also become part of the lakeshore family.

"*Over the years since we moved in, most of the cottages around us have become year-round residences for their owners. We're at our cottage quite often, so that means we've had the opportunity to get to know our neighbors. We've become part of a special community on the Lakeshore, and we feel right at home.*"

— *Jack and Barbara Weigle*

"My roots are on the lakeshore, and I enjoy being part of the community in this area. Clients appreciate that we know the area and can help them get involved."
— Ross

ONE WAY

DO NOT

ENTER

99

"You can't get a better spot to see the harbor and watch the summer events go on."

Family Name
The Newpols

Needs
A manageable vacation experience for a young family

Passions
Family Time, Local Festivals and Attractions

Location
South Haven

Jon and Sherri Newpol's Story

Dream

We live in Ann Arbor, Michigan, on the east side of the state. We had taken our three young boys on various beach vacations, and they really enjoyed them, but it was almost too much of a hassle at times to figure out where to go, get everything packed, get everyone on the plane, and then deal with a touristy environment. We looked into homes on one of the many small lakes in the general vicinity, but we loved the ocean-like feel of Lake Michigan. At approximately two hours from our home, it would be a much more manageable travel experience that we wouldn't dread. We were convinced that the Lake Michigan coast was the place to look.

Location and Decision

We didn't envision building at first, so we were looking at the available inventory. We didn't have a particular community in mind, so we looked all up and down the Southwest Michi-gan lakeshore. We noticed that some homes were much higher quality than others. Many homes showed signs that the harsh weather of the lakeshore was taking its toll. We were concerned that these homes would take an additional investment to make them nice places to live again. But other homes were evidently of higher quality, so we asked our realtor about the builders. Cottage Home was one builder that clearly put out quality work. We even found one of their homes that we liked, but it didn't meet our needs.

When we couldn't find any houses that met our needs, we started looking at lots. There were a handful we were interested in, but two side-by-side lots in South Haven near the beach and the river especially intrigued us. They had more of the amenities that were of interest to us. There's a street and a marina between the lots and the river, and they're a hundred yards from the beach. There was also a total view of the river.

"The Cottage Home team came up with an initial design that blew us away. It was creative, it optimized the lot and the views of the water, and it seemed like it would stand the test of time. We moved a few things around, and they were great about immediately responding with revised drawings. It was the most enjoyable home purchasing and building experience we've ever had."

Location and Decision, continued

We called up Cottage Home and asked them if they would check out the lots and tell us if they could build on them. Brian ended up looking at both lots, and he offered to buy the second lot and build another Cottage Home on it. We agreed, and the process was off to a great start.

Design and Build

The design process was actually a lot of fun. We gave Cottage Home a whole wish list, including styles, how many rooms we wanted, layout, how we wanted to use the cottage, and as much information as we could think of about our family and our preferences. We made a big deal about it being beach friendly, since we knew we would have sandy kids coming in and out with two dogs. We also knew that we wanted to take advantage of the view of the river.

The Cottage Home team came up with an initial design that blew us away. It was creative, it optimized the lot and the views of the water, and it seemed like it would stand the test of time. We basically just tweaked it. We moved a few things around, and they were great about immediately responding with revised drawings.

This was the most enjoyable home purchasing and building experience we've ever had. Cottage Home built our house up off the ground a bit so you can view the river and downtown area from the porch. There's also a screened-in, rounded porch with great views. We spend the most time there as a family. On top of that is a deck with beautiful views of town, including the festivals and fireworks. It's the envy of South Haven.

Life on the Lakeshore

We live a really hectic lifestyle, and we don't get to spend a lot of time together most days. We divide and conquer, rushing the kids around. But our cottage has become the place where we all go to take a deep breath and hang out together. It's the only place where we actually sit around the table and eat together, play baseball and football, kayak, and paddle board. We were worried that we wouldn't be able to spend time as a family while the kids were growing up, but our cottage has made that possible.

Community

This isn't a private area, so in some ways our cottage is very different from other Cottage Homes. Our house is in a historic downtown area, and we were initially worried that it wouldn't fit Cottage Home's model. But they actually do a diverse array of building, so they had no problem making our cottage work.

All the things that people get sold on about the lakeshore towns really are as great as everyone says they are. We have access to festivals, wine country, fireworks, and more. The people of South Haven are just nice people, and it's a great place to hang out. It was important to us that the house would be beautiful, since our neighbors worry about everything that gets built because it will affect their views and property values. But Cottage Home worked really hard to be polite and fit into the neighborhood. It made our neighbors proud to have us join their community. It really helped us to be welcomed, and we're very grateful for that.

"The winter we built the Newpols' home was the coldest it's ever been when I've built a house. They were pouring concrete in negative degrees. That whole process was incredibly freezing. But now it's an awesome place in South Haven. You can't get a better spot to see the harbor and watch the summer events go on."

—Eric

"The design process was actually a lot of fun."

"The design process was actually a lot of fun. We gave Cottage Home a whole wish list, including styles, how many rooms we wanted, layout, how we wanted to use the cottage, and as much information as we could think of about our family and our preferences."

Newpol Family Cottage Profile

Jon and Sherri were longtime fans of Cottage Home who watched them for a while, then called them to do their project when they found property in the Harbor District of South Haven. Cottage Home built both the Newpols' cottage and a second house on the vacant lot next door, which they rented as a vacation spot for a while and eventually sold.

"Cottage Home built our house up off the ground a bit so you can view the river and downtown area from the porch. There's also a screened-in, rounded porch with great views. We spend the most time there as a family. On top of that is a deck with beautiful views of town, including the festivals and fireworks. It's the envy of South Haven."

"John and Sherri picked out their site before Cottage Home got in-volved, and it turned out that their property had unstable soil. When we found out we were already committed to the project, and it looked like it was going to be extremely expensive to fix. We circled the wag-ons, reengineered things, figured out a sensible, economical solution that was half of the original estimated cost, and then talked to the Newpols. We ended up splitting the cost with them. Thankfully, we were still able to make their project work."

– Jeremy

The Newpol Cottage

Cottage Home
Designers & Builders of
Well-Appointed Beach Houses & Cottages

PLAN APPROVAL

BY SIGNING HERE AND INITIALING SUBSEQUENT PAGES BUYER APPROVES THE PLANS AND SPECIFICATIONS FOR THE HOME AND ACKNOWLEDGES THE FOLLOWING: ALL PLANS AND SPECIFICATIONS ARE SUBJECT TO SUBSTITUTION BY COTTAGE HOME WITHOUT NOTICE TO BUYER AS LONG AS THE CHANGE OR SUBSTITUTION DOES NOT MATERIALLY AFFECT THE VALUE OF THE PROPERTY. FURTHERMORE, ALL ADDITIONAL USE, DUPLICATION, PUBLICATION, SALE, OR DISTRIBUTION OF PLANS WITHOUT PERMISSION BY COTTAGE HOME REPRESENTS A VIOLATION OF FEDERAL COPYRIGHT LAW AND IS SUBJECT TO LEGAL PROCEDURES AND PENALTIES.

COTTAGE HOME   DATE

SIGNED   DATE

SIGNED   DATE

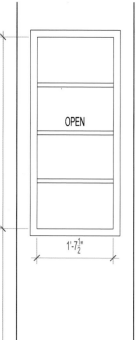

OPEN

1'-7 1/2"

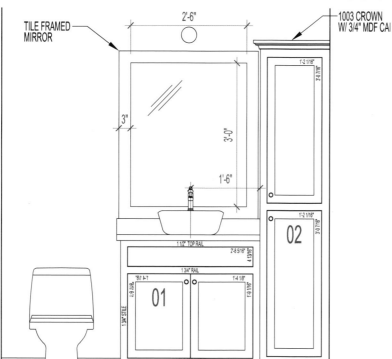

TILE FRAMED MIRROR

2'-6"

1003 CROWN W/ 3/4" MDF CAI

3"

3'-0"

1'-6"

1-2 1/16"

3'-0 7/16"

1-2 1/16"

3'-0 7/16"

02

1 1/2" TOP RAIL

2-8 5/16"

1 3/4" RAIL

1'-4 1/8"

01

"We made a big deal about it being beach friendly, since we knew we would have sandy kids coming in and out with two dogs. We also knew that we wanted to take advantage of the view of the river."

Beach Access and Bluff Patios

Much of the southwest coastline of Lake Michigan features high bluffs and dunes. They create beautiful spots to build cottages overlooking the lake. Many properties have stairways winding down the bluff to provide beach access. Others take advantage of these scenic overlooks by building patios on the bluff. Occasionally, if they can do it in a way that's sensitive to the natural environment, Cottage Home has even re-contoured the bluff to give homeowners more direct access to the lake.

"We're glad we were convinced to re-contour the bluff, because it allowed Cottage Home to do everything that they've done on our property."

— *Guy and Barb Calhoun*

"Our cottage is up on the bluff, and there are sixty-three stairs in four levels that take you down to the shore. Cottage Home reshaped the bluff so it wouldn't fall away. We're very impressed by their commitment to the environment."

— *Jane and Steve Marks*

The Lakeshore Community

"We know that people are coming here for the beach and the surrounding community, so we do everything we can to make them better. We love to celebrate what's good about the area."

— Brian

"My roots are on the lakeshore, and I enjoy being part of the community in this area. Clients appreciate that we know the area and can help them get involved."

— Ross

"Southwest Michigan is a family-oriented area with lots to do. It has great downtowns and vibrant communities. It's a great place to live and work, and I can certainly see why after searching for a vacation home, sometimes for many years, people would make this their destination."

— Stephanie

"We hold some sort of Cottage Home event every summer, to which we invite all of our past clients. We've hosted summer socials and parties at various community locations, and we always have local restaurants cater the events. We want our clients to experience all the things that make West Michigan such a great place to vacation."

— Stephanie

The Small Town Feel

"We love the restaurants in town. Everyone is so friendly—it's so different from Illinois. In South Haven, I feel like everyone knows us. It has that small town feel. When we go out to dinner, the owners of the restaurants know my kids' names, and my kids love that. They feel like they're special, almost like celebrities, because of that small town feel. It's a different speed, a little slower. You take in a little more and enjoy simpler things, which we appreciate, and we appreciate that our kids get to experience what it's like to live in a small town. It's great for them to have that kind of exposure; otherwise, they wouldn't even know that it existed. We were so pleasantly surprised. Even when you go to the grocery store, everyone's just so friendly and nice. It's a completely different feel than the city."

— Anthony and Jenny Iaderosa

"*All the things that people get sold on about the lakeshore towns really are as great as everyone says they are. We have access to festivals, wine country, fireworks, and more. The people of South Haven are just nice people, and it's a great place to hang out.*"

— Jon and Sherri Newpol

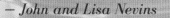

"*We'd never lived in a small town before, and it's been fun to come here and get to know the people who live here. It's kind of fun to learn to live in a small town. Our suburb in Chicago isn't that big, but it's part of a megapolis. But up there you're part of a small community, and you can actually get to know people.*"

— John and Lisa Nevins

Steve Kloosterhouse

Lead Carpentry and Finishes

"I love hands-on work. I'm actually a fourth generation carpenter. The opportunity to use my gifts that way gets me excited every day. My wife says, 'I can't believe how excited you are to go to work.' I get to be creative, I get to do what I love to do, and I work on amazing things. I get to do this— it's my privilege. And it's not just the work itself—I also love the people that I work with."

"*I am the lead carpenter at Cottage Home. I do carpentry work, but I also manage the other carpenters. When it comes to the finish carpentry, that's when my role really gets intense.*"

"*We care for each other at Cottage Home, and that fits into my values and who I am. Being a part of the whole is so exciting, especially when we get done. The finished houses are so cool.*"

Legacy

"We love it when family comes to visit. We have five grandkids, and they simply adore the beach. This is a wonderful place to spend our retirement, and we're excited to share the Lake Michigan shoreline with our friends and family far into the future."

— Guy and Barb Calhoun

Legacy

Your lakeshore cottage isn't just about the present—it's about the future, too. Beach homes become gathering places for friends and family, destinations that everyone can share and places where fond memories are made. Often, they're places that remain in one family for generations. Most Cottage Home clients pursue their dreams of owning a home on the Big Lake to create a spot of reprieve, where friends and family can get away and enjoy the beach—and just being together.

A number of the cottages we've built are designed around the desire to make a weekend (or week) spent at grandma and grandpa's the best it can be. Other owners of Lake Michigan cottages build them with their retirement in mind, planning to move in full-time once they have the chance.

A spot for family reunions and beach parties with friends, or a quiet retirement getaway—however you use your Cottage Home, it will create a legacy that will be appreciated for generations to come.

"In the future, we anticipate passing our cottage on to the family so that even more generations of Weigles can enjoy it. The older grandkids are already talking about bringing their kids here when they have them. We're saving all the toys for our great-grandchildren! Simply put, the cottage is an anchor spot for the whole family, and we're overjoyed to leave that legacy."

— Jack and Barbara Weigle

Cottage Home designed and built this porch to honor Barbara's desire to have a porch modeled after the long, magnificent front porch at the Grand Hotel on Mackinac Island.

Family Name	Location
The Weigles	Holland

Features	Passions
Lower-Level Walkout, Bunk Room, Front Porch	Grandkids, Hockey

Jack and Barbara Weigle's Story

Dream

When our children were young, we would often bring them to the beach to get away from the busyness of life. Jack's work as a physician was demanding, but his days off provided our family with an opportunity to escape. Sometimes we would rent cottages on inland lakes so we could teach the kids to swim and row. It had always been Barbara's dream to live on the shores of the Big Lake, so we started to incorporate house hunting into our day trips to the beach.

Location

As we were driving on the lakeshore one day, we stumbled upon a cottage on a beautiful stretch of beach in a lovely neighborhood in Holland. The cottage was nearly a hundred years old and in bad shape, but this was the first place that Barbara had really fallen in love with. We decided to buy the cottage with a plan in mind: if we didn't like it after five years, we'd sell it.

Well, five years went by, and we only fell more deeply in love with the cottage and the lakeshore. It was everything we loved about our vacations on the beach, but better. It was nearly impossible for Jack to relax with the demands of his work, but things were different at the cottage. He could feel his stress level going down only halfway through the drive to get there! At the cottage, Jack felt like he could actually sit in a chair and read a book, or cut the grass, rake the leaves, or even just relax and listen to the sound of the waves. It was so quiet on the Big Lake, unlike the smaller lakes where we had rented cottages before. Spending time at the cottage was so relaxing that that after only two years, Jack decided to cancel his membership at the golf club. He didn't need it anymore!

"Barbara told Brian that she wanted a long porch on the house like the one on the Grand Hotel on Mackinac Island. Jack almost fell off his chair! 'I want one like it, but smaller,' said Barbara. 'How much smaller?' asked Jack! In the end, we did get a porch just like the Grand Hotel's, though it is quite a bit smaller!"

Decision

But even though we loved our old cottage, we couldn't deny that it was falling apart. Plus, our family was growing with a fifth grandchild on the way, and space in the cottage was limited. It was time to build something new. We talked to a few architects recommended by friends, but none of them worked out. They wanted to build the cottage their way, not our way. We also had issues with the surveyor and the Department of Environmental Quality, who told us they had to build much further back from the lake than we wanted. After months of this we were so discouraged that we started looking for another property, even though we knew nothing could beat our current location and the tight-knit surrounding community.

All this time, we were actually friends with Brian and his family, unaware of Brian's work with Cottage Home. For several years they had sat across the aisle from us at Griffins hockey games, and we had watched each others' children grow up. Then, by utter coincidence, Barbara found out that the solution to our problem had been right under our noses all along! We invited Brian to take a look at the cottage, and he was able to correct the previous surveyor just by eyeballing the property. We were impressed by Brian's knowledge, and we were starting to get excited about designing a new cottage.

Design and Build

We met with Brian several times to talk about what we wanted in our new cottage. Brian already knew our story, but he wanted to know more about how we envisioned living in the new place. Brian knew how to ask the right questions about our lifestyle so he could come up with a layout that would facilitate it. He was perceptive and picked up on small details, incorporating them into the plans. Our family had already clicked with Brian's family, and our friendship only deepened as we worked together on our cottage. Our family also clicked with the rest of the team at Cottage Home, finding them to be both knowledgeable and friendly. We like to think of the Cottage Home team as a big family, but without the usual squabbles! We live in nearby Grandville, so during the building process we were able to be very involved, visiting the property every week. We enjoyed checking up on progress, and the team seemed to enjoy spending time with us, too.

Move-In

Before we knew it, we were moving furniture into the cottage and talking about who we would have join us on our first night staying there. We have two sons with a daughter in between, so it was obvious that our daughter would get the honor! (Not really, but the boys like to give her a hard time.) We decided to make a special family event out of it. That first weekend our three children and their spouses came out to the cottage, and their kids all stayed with their other grandparents for the night. We had a steak dinner together, and then the six of them all slept in the bunk room. Imagine that—six adults, sleeping in bunk beds! They still talk about it to this day. In the morning we had a big breakfast, and then they all went and picked up their kids and came back to spend the day on the beach. All three generations were there for this special beach day, and we still talk about it ten years later! We all felt so fortunate and blessed.

Aftercare

Cottage Home didn't abandon our family after the cottage was finished, either. We recently had a question about our deck, and Brian came out personally to figure out what the issue was and how to fix it. It turned out that the three-season room needed to be jacked up a little bit. It wasn't a very noticeable problem, but he wanted to make sure it was fixed before it became a major issue.

"The Weigles were really nostalgic going into the construction process. Their fireplace sticks out in my mind. They wanted to recreate one that was in their existing cottage."

—Doug

"It was a stroke of genius!"

When the Weigles moved into their Cottage Home in 2006, they took a photo of their grandchildren having a sleepover in the bunk room. Then in 2012, six years later, they sent us another photo of their grandkids at the cottage. Time flies when you're having fun!

"The panorama is truly something to behold."

"We always call our cottage 'The Cottage,' never a 'house' or a 'home.' That's because we wanted it to feel like a beach getaway and a special vacation spot, not just another house. Brian and the team picked up on this, and when the cottage was finished they gave us a sign that says 'The Cottage.' We found it on our mantle with a note thanking us for letting Cottage Home build it!"

Life on the Lakeshore

Some of our friends have built lake homes that look like regular houses, and they didn't even take advantage of the view in the way they placed their windows. Their houses could be anywhere—there's nothing special about them that makes them Lake Michigan beach cottages. We wanted the complete opposite of that, and we got what we'd always dreamed of. Even though we come year-round, we've preserved the feel of a cottage. Cottage Home helped us create the right look and feel, and the way they placed our windows means we have spectacular views in every part of our cottage. The panorama is truly something to behold, and it changes throughout the year, never growing old or boring. We love to watch the weather over the lake, everything from dramatic storms to tranquil sunsets.

Community

Over the years since we moved in, most of the cottages around us have become year-round residences for their owners. We're at our cottage quite often, so that means we've had the opportunity to get to know our neighbors. We've become part of a special community on the lakeshore, and we feel right at home.

Legacy

Overall, our cottage is very kid-friendly and family-friendly, which is exactly what we wanted and needed. We'll have two of our kids' families over at a time, and we have Thanksgiving and Christmas celebrations with our whole extended family at the cottage. Our older grandkids are in high school and college, and they'll call us up and ask if they can bring their friends up for a beach day. They want their friends to be here because they had such a great experience of the cottage growing up. Our four-year-old grandson was at a state park beach in Ludington not long ago, and he asked his parents, "What are all these people doing here?"

Our grandkids had a nice private beach to go to all the time, and they got used to it!

Last year, we wanted to do a photo with our entire extended family, so we tried to find a day that everyone could do it. In June, July, and August there was just one day that everyone could make! That meant we had to pull it off regardless of what the weather was like, and it was one of our extremely windy days on the lakeshore. Our sheltered patio came in handy, and we were able to get a photo with everyone in our family.

In the future, we anticipate passing our cottage on to the family so that even more generations of Weigles can enjoy it. The older grandkids are already talking about bringing their kids here when they have them. We're saving all the toys for our great-grandchildren! Simply put, the cottage is an anchor spot for the whole family, and we're overjoyed to leave that legacy.

"I was surprised to find out that Jack Weigle delivered me—he was my mom's OB/GYN! I was telling my mom about these clients we were working with, and she told me, 'You've met him before!'"

—Jeremy

"Barbara told Brian that she liked the idea of angled walls to add visual interest to the cottage's interior. Cottage Home pulled that off wonderfully."

Weigle Family Cottage Profile

The Weigles' cottage is designed to take full advantage of their magnificent views of the lake and to facilitate frequent visits from their grandkids.

"Jack wanted to keep two windows from the old cottage, so Brian saved them and put mirrors in them. Once they were hanging in our cottage, Brian told us to take a look. With the way he had placed the mirrored windows, you could see the reflection of the lake in them when you walk in the front door. It was a stroke of genius!"

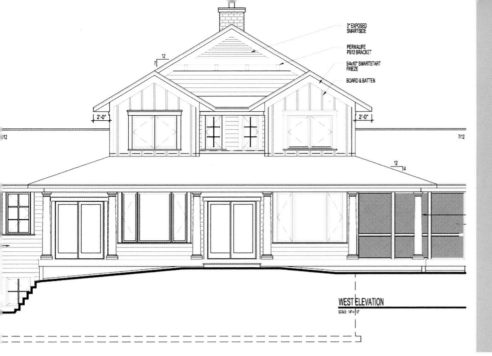

WEST ELEVATION
SCALE: 1/4"=1'-0"

"We told Brian that our family needed an area for the grandkids to come in without tracking sand through the whole house. We would also need a source of warm water to hose off the kids before they came inside. Brian designed a lower-level walkout that's perfect for kids coming back from the beach. The outdoor shower even has the warm water we wanted, plus a bath right inside the doors."

"The cottages we build are generational. They're built with family in mind, both now and in the future."

— Dirk

The Weigles' Fireplace

"Barbara really wanted to save the original fireplace from our old cottage. We talked to Brian about it, and he looked into it, but it turned out not to be feasible. That was the only time they ever said no to us! Barbara got teary-eyed when they knocked down our beloved fireplace, but Brian put his arm around her and said, "Don't worry—I'll build you another one just like it. I promise." And they built an exact replica in our new cottage! Barbara loves it, and it's the perfect centerpiece for our dining room and living room area. It was things like this that showed us just how much the Cottage Home team cared about what we wanted and the small details that were important to us."

— Jack and Barbara Weigle

"Cottage Home was great about adding in nice finishing touches when they gave us the keys to our new cottage. For one, there's their signature porch swing that they give to every family they work with. They asked us where we wanted it, and the front porch seemed ideal, but we get so much wind off the lake there that it really wasn't the right spot. So they chose to put it on our patio, which they had specifically designed to be sheltered from the wind. Perfect!"

— Jack and Barbara Weigle

Cottage Home

Porch Swings

Porch swings are one of Cottage Home's specialties. When you live on the beautiful shores of Lake Michigan, there's nothing quite like relaxing on a porch swing at the end of the day, watching the sun set over the lake. Other swings hang on front porches and provide a perfect spot to read a book or the morning newspaper. Wherever the swing is located, it's sure to be an incredible spot to take in the views and swing your cares away.

Joel Wondergem

Architectural Drafting and Rendering

"My role is a little bit of everything, but primarily I'm in the office doing AutoCAD drawings, putting Brian's basic hand-drawn designs into the computer to make it more real. That makes the next step of getting estimates more accurate. I also do LEED documentation and keep that process moving continuously. I do a little bit of field work as well, including tile."

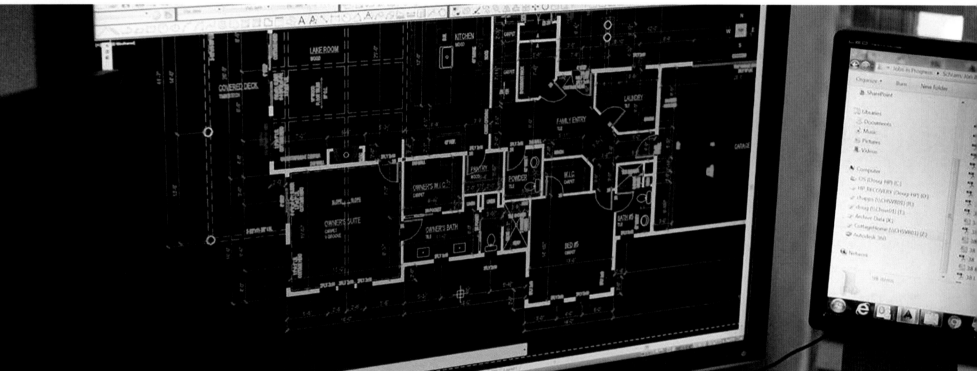

"The lakeshore matters to me, and the creativity of our work is important to me. The houses are all different. I'm an artist at heart, so the ever-changing design process is a big deal to me. It's a lot of fun. Every house and every site is unique. Seeing the results is very cool."

Holland

Holland combines small town friendliness and charm with a big helping of Lake Michigan beauty. Try visiting Big Red Lighthouse at the state park, or stop by Lake Macatawa to go boating or to take a stroll down the boardwalk. Downtown Holland offers excellent shopping and dining options, as well as several local breweries. Don't miss De Zwaan, the only authentic, working Dutch windmill in the United States. In May, you can join people from all over the world as they flock to Holland for Tulip Time. And with everything from golf courses to blueberry farms, the surrounding area offers memorable attractions year-round.

"The Holland area has so much to offer. We make sure to pick up pamphlets on attractions so our guests won't get bored. It's great being able to run out to Holland for dinner in the evening, and then come back to the cottage for the sunset."

— Phil and Lynn Kennedy

"Our cottage is in a lovely neighborhood on a beautiful stretch of beach in Holland. It's a quiet, friendly neighborhood, and we've loved getting to know our neighbors and the area. We've become part of a special community on the lakeshore, and we feel right at home."

— Jack and Barbara Weigle

The Cottage Home Family

"We like to think of the Cottage Home team as a big family, but without the usual squabbles!"

— Jack and Barbara Weigle

"Everyone I work with I consider a friend. There's nobody I don't like working with."

— Josh

"We're almost a family. We're all on the same page, and we all care. We're not just here to do a job and punch out at 5:00. Countless times you hear guys saying that they were lying awake at night thinking about the job. How many people do that? Or they'll go out to the site and double check on things to make sure they're right. The care and concern that goes into the house defines who we are. Everyone has their little part in it, and together it really blends well."

—Joel

Acknowledgements

Life on the Lakeshore started out as a hard copy version of the Cottage Home experience. But in the end, it turned out to be much more than that. It became a book of stories, nine beautiful stories about special families at meaningful places on the shore. We are so grateful to these families for inviting us into the screened-in porches of their lives. We were not surprised by the passion with which they spoke of their cottages, but we are humbled by their gracious comments. Thank you, families.

Now comes the difficult part. I want to apologize to all of the hundred or so clients whose stories are not featured in this book. We love all of our Cottage Home owners and wish we could have included everyone's story, but of course we couldn't fit them all. Perhaps we'll come up with a *Life on the Lakeshore: Part II* someday. The next time you see me out and about on the lakeshore, remind me of this and I'll take you out for dinner.

This book also tells the story of remarkable people who individually are lights in this world, and who together make a bright beam. When the Cottage Home team focuses their efforts together, they are truly a beam on the horizon, and they will find what they are looking for. I am so grateful to and proud of this family, which includes Jeremy van Eyk, Doug Postema, Stephanie Bauman, Ross Brown, Wendy Spoelhof, Eric Leatherberry, Joel Wondergem, Steve Kloosterhouse, Justin Lambers, Karl Price, Josh Kuhn, and Dirk Bronsink.

We'd be remiss if we didn't mention a few longtime Cottage Home team members whose efforts contributed greatly to many of the outstanding homes pictured in this book. Vicki Zylstra, Dave VanOrder, and Jennifer Klaassen spent a combined total of thirty-five years with our team, and they helped make us who we are today.

While they have moved on to pursue other endeavors, we continue to be grateful for their contributions of time and talent, and we wish them all the best.

We would also like to thank the greater Cottage Home team. We would not be able to do what we do without the many vendors, trade contractors, and experts who are all part of the homes we create. Your commitment, artisanship, and passion are appreciated.

Thank you as well to the team at Black Lake Studio, including Greg Smith, Cory Lakatos, Ashley Helminiak, and Caraline Visuri. Together, we have done great work with sensitivity and diligence. Your interviews with families and team members were purposeful and fun. From a builder of cottages to a builder of books, I say job well done.

Finally, we wish to say thank you to all of our lakeshore neighbors, leaders, advocates, chefs, shop owners, growers, and lakeshore fans. We learned long ago that our clients don't come here because we build cool cottages. They come here because it's a special place. Thanks to all who celebrate, every day, what is right about Southwest Michigan, and continue to make it better.

The story doesn't end here, though. There are many more lakeshore stories to be created and told. If you would like to connect with us, please check us out at cottagehome.com. You are also welcome to email me (brian@cottagehome.com) or call me on my mobile phone anytime (616.886.1840).

Once again, it is with sincere gratitude to all the clients and friends of Cottage Home that we say thank you. Because of you, we are living the dream.

Brian Bosgraaf
Cottage Home President and Designer

Photo Acknowledgements

Dan Johnson Photography

Justin Lambers

Murdoch Marketing

Abbyjeanne Photography

Jennifer Waters Photography

Cottage Home

Designers & Builders of
Well-Appointed Beach Houses & Cottages